AF418425

HEALING WITHOUT SHAME

DR. WILLIAMETTA SIMMONS

Scripture quotations are taken from the Holy Bible, New International Version®, NIV®. Copyright © 1973, 1978, 1984, 2011 by Biblica, Inc. Used with permission of Zondervan. All rights reserved worldwide. www.zondervan.com.

This book is intended for informational and educational purposes only. It is not a substitute for professional mental health treatment, medical advice, or crisis intervention. If you or someone you know is in crisis, please contact a licensed mental health professional or call a crisis helpline immediately.

All stories and case examples shared in this book are used with permission or have been altered to protect the privacy and identity of the individuals involved. Any resemblance to specific persons, living or deceased, is coincidental unless expressly noted.

Cover and interior formatting by KUHN Design Group | kuhndesigngroup.com

Copyediting by Janelle DeBlaay

Healing Without Shame:
Faith, Mental Health, and the Courage to Be Honest
Copyright © 2026 by Williametta Simmons, PsyD, MBA

All rights reserved. No part of this publication may be reproduced, distributed, or transmitted in any form or by any means, including photocopying, recording, or other electronic or mechanical methods, without the prior written permission of the author, except in the case of brief quotations embodied in critical reviews and certain other noncommercial uses permitted by copyright law.

Published by Integrative Psychological & Consulting Services, LLC

First Edition

Printed in the United States of America

DEDICATION

To my mother, Pastor Phanta Kamara.

Your life is a living testimony of strength rooted in faith, courage refined through adversity, and love poured out through sacrifice. In seasons that demanded more than seemed possible, you remained steadfast. You carried burdens quietly and with dignity so our family could rise. Your grace under pressure shaped the woman I have become, and your example is the quiet engine behind this work.

To my husband, Alexander Sonpon Jr., my partner and greatest champion, thank you for loving me patiently, listening to every "grand" idea, and standing beside me through each step of this journey. Your strength, kindness, and steady encouragement have been a covering throughout this process.

To my dearest friend, Hadassah (Esther) Orega, you believed when I wavered. You stood firm when I wanted to quit. You carried courage for both of us and would not allow doubt to bow my head. You prayed me through every page, reminding me that I am a gift to the body of Christ, called not only to speak encouragement, but to write it. This book bears your fingerprints of faith. I am forever grateful for you.

To my birth country, Liberia, my heart and my heritage, through your soil I learned strength; through your history, humility; and through your people, resilience. My passion for mental wellness is rooted in the personal and collective wounds of the Liberian Civil War, and in the enduring hope of a people who continue to courageously heal.

To America, the land of promise and possibility, thank you for opening your doors to an immigrant child and giving her space to dream, to grow, and to become.

And to every soul who has entrusted me with their stories, their wounds, and their healing, this book exists because of your courage. May these pages remind you that you are seen, valued, and never alone.

Regrettably, many Christians have adopted toxic ideas about suffering wherein it becomes associated with shame and spiritual failure. Dr. Simmons, relying on the words of Scripture and a close reading of the spiritual themes from the life and work of Jesus, provides a needed corrective to these misconceptions. Health care professionals, whether Christian or not, can find value in reading this book.

—**Dr. Samuel Knapp**, retired psychologist

As both a pre-licensed psychotherapist and lead pastor, I have witnessed first-hand the damage caused when faith communities confuse spiritual devotion with emotional denial. *Healing Without Shame* confronts that harm with uncommon honesty, clinical wisdom, and Christ-centered compassion, offering a faithful path forward that honors both mental health and spiritual integrity. Dr. Williametta Simmons gives the church a necessary language for presence rather than performance—and a vision of healing rooted in truth, dignity, and grace.

—**Rev. S. Gentry Taylor**, Lead Pastor,
Philadelphia Church International—Minnesota;
pre-licensed psychotherapist & mental health specialist

Healing Without Shame speaks with equal clarity to the one seeking healing and the one offering it. Dr. Simmons reveals the gap between the church as a perceived space of healing and the wounded who approach it—and issues a clear call to emulate Jesus, who embraced everyone regardless of race, color, creed, past, or trauma. This book is essential reading for every pastor ready to adopt a new spiritual posture for healing the saints.

—**Rev. Editus Addy I, MSW**, Pastor, Agape
International Outreach Ministries

ACKNOWLEDGMENTS

First and foremost, I give thanks to God for fresh revelation and deeper understanding surrounding mental health. I thank Him for the assurance that "A bruised reed he will not break, and a smoldering wick he will not snuff out, till he has brought justice through to victory" (Matthew 12:20). This promise is a tender reminder that God cares for us in every condition (physical, mental, and spiritual) and that His compassion meets us gently in our fragility.

To my parents, Reverend Dr. C. William Simmons and Reverend Dr. Marie Simmons, thank you for your prayers, wisdom, and unwavering guidance. Your faithfulness and leadership have shaped my life in ways I will forever honor. I am deeply grateful that God chose you to be my parents.

To my pastors Apostle Samuel B. Martin Jr., Juah Martin, Pastor Dr. Percy Bland, and Dr. LaFaye Bland, thank you for modeling excellence in God's Kingdom. Your humility, integrity, compassion, and grace have provided steady spiritual covering and continual inspiration.

To my older sisters Nadia Kehzie and Farmetta Simmons-Garbla, thank you for being extraordinary big sisters. You strengthen me, champion me, and believe in me even in moments when I struggle to believe in myself. That gift is priceless.

To my siblings Ruthie Simmons, Christian "Billy" Simmons, Grace Simmons, Martin Dorliae, and Konnah Anderson, thank you for the joy, love, and strength you bring into my life. I cherish each of you deeply.

To my friends Cinthia, Onyx, Jeta, Jane, Latrese, and Deborah, I am profoundly grateful to walk through life with women of such compassion, brilliance, and loyalty. Thank you for standing with me through trials and triumphs, tears and celebration, and every sacred season in between.

To the women of Growing Together in Love (G.T.I.L.), Mispa, Brenda (Yah), Akilah, Dolly, Maryah, and Tomah, thank you for the gift of true sisterhood. Your encouragement, laughter, and love have strengthened me more than you know.

To the Liberia Medical Mission team, thank you for welcoming me into such a remarkable humanitarian family. Our work continues to transform lives in the United States, West Africa, and beyond. Through this mission, I have witnessed firsthand that there is no greater ministry and no deeper fulfillment than serving those in need.

Finally, to my extended family, friends, and loved ones, thank you for the countless ways you have shaped and supported my journey. Because of you, I continue to grow, to strive, and to hope.

With abiding gratitude.

CONTENTS

Why, my soul, are you downcast?
Why so disturbed within me?
Put your hope in God, for I will yet
praise him, my Savior and my God.

PSALM 43:5

FOREWORD

BY PASTOR G. THOMAS DOWIE

In 2003, during a violent episode of the Liberian Civil War, I called a friend across town to check on her. As gunfire erupted, I found myself trapped and uncertain about what to do next. When my friend asked if I was alright, I replied that I was fine. She responded, "No, you are not fine. You are stressed." Her words led me to a new awareness of my own mental state. At the time, I was unfamiliar with the concept of stress, even the word itself.

As a teenager, I faced rejection at home, and as an adult, I lived through years of war. Over time, my instinct to survive made suffering feel normal to me. It should have been obvious that I was depressed, being trapped in a war. But for me the violence of the war was just an external version of the internal turbulence I have always lived with. I didn't realize I was struggling with my mental health, especially since mental health services were not available.

Now, as a husband, parent, and pastor, in hindsight the cost of surviving with mental weights, emotional fractures, and psychological disruptions that I couldn't identify or articulate is beyond measure. My culture and church community did not acknowledge these issues. And any mention of mental health was viewed as a spiritual attack requiring prayer. Only God knows the pain, disappointments, and unintended mistakes I made. How I wish that the insights in this book were available to me then! Sadly, many others have faced even greater hardships.

Mental health is now a defining concern of our time. Anxiety, depression, emotional exhaustion, and trauma affect nearly every family, church, and workplace. The fast-paced world of the 21st century and increasing isolation, especially of Western society, further exacerbate the crisis. For many years, discussions about mental and emotional wellness were misunderstood, minimized, ignorantly despised, or avoided within Christian communities.

Dr. Williametta Simmons addresses this gap with a strong Christian background and extensive professional experience, fostering a conversation marked by clarity, compassion, and conviction. Her personal experiences with grief, loss, and betrayal, combined with her Christian upbringing and expertise as a practicing psychologist, give her unique credibility on this subject.

The need for an all-encompassing approach to the human person cannot be exaggerated. Humans are tripartite in composition. Every individual embodies a spirit, soul, and body, intricately interwoven by God—hence the need for a holistic approach to meeting human needs.

The complexity of psychological health is shaped not only by human nature but also by cultural, social, and political factors. These influences expose individuals to trauma, violence, and various forms of abuse, contributing to mental health challenges.

The story of the Bible itself is dotted with accounts of individuals from virtually every conceivable sector of society who wrestled with emotional crisis. The books of Psalms and Lamentations narrate the anguish suffered by people mightily used by God. David was, on many occasions, overwhelmed by intense pressure (Psalm 28:1; 61:2). Job cursed the day that he was born and regretted that he didn't die in stillbirth (Job 3). Jeremiah accused God of taking advantage of him (Jeremiah 20:7–9). Elijah collapsed in exhaustion and despair (1 Kings 19:10). Even our Lord Jesus, the Almighty God in human flesh, was not spared the trouble of mental crisis. His time in the garden of Gethsemane and wailing over Jerusalem's unbelief were moments of profound anguish of the soul. History tells about the debilitating depression that the great Reformer Martin Luther suffered. The death of the 19th-century iconic preacher Charles Spurgeon might have been partly because of the persistent depression he endured.

These accounts remind us that mental health struggles are not spiritual failures. Instead, they highlight the complexity of human life and its emotional challenges. Elijah asked God to take his life under the weight of emotional burden, and David nearly resorted to violence after Nabal's refusal, likely influenced by Saul's earlier attacks.

In her book, Dr. Simmons breaks down the barrier between spirituality and psychological understanding. She demonstrates that mental health care is a credible ministry of faith. Psychology deepens human understanding and complements faith. When approached with wisdom, psychological insights can illuminate aspects of the human condition already recognized in Scripture.

This book assures readers that Christian mental health does not replace faith with therapy or reduce spirituality to clinical methods. Instead, it integrates biblical truth, emotional awareness, and practical wisdom to promote genuine, lasting healing. Since faith is rooted in belief, and belief is a mental force, a healthier mind supports stronger faith.

The following pages guide readers through this integration, challenging misconceptions, offering thoughtful guidance, and providing hope for those overwhelmed by inner struggles. Most importantly, they affirm that God's care for us includes restoring our minds and hearts.

This work offers strong encouragement and valuable insight for pastors, counselors, leaders, and believers who care for others. It shows that seeking help, strengthening emotional health, and cultivating the mind are not departures from faith but acts of faithful stewardship.

I hope this book encourages honest conversations within Christian communities and provides a framework for understanding faith and mental health as partners in the pursuit of wholeness. May this be the beginning of intentionally integrating mental health services into the framework of spiritual ministry.

May the principles so excellently articulated in Dr. Simmons's book inspire many to begin a journey of emotional healing and resilience, embracing this sacred duty, with God's help, to restore the broken-hearted and bind up their wounds.

G. Thomas Dowie
Lead Pastor—Kingdom Restoration Ministries, International
Mentor Partner of Halas Co-Xel, a marketplace training
program for Christian professionals
MARCH 15, 2026

INTRODUCTION

*"I didn't tell anyone at church I was depressed.
I thought if I prayed more or fasted more, it would go
away. But it didn't. I was afraid they would judge
me and think my faith wasn't strong enough."*

These are the words of a Christian who loved the Lord sincerely but suffered silently. Sadly, they are not alone.

For more than a decade, I have heard similar stories from people struggling with their mental health who felt afraid to speak up because of stigma in the church. I heard them as a psychologist. I heard them as a ministry leader. And eventually, I heard them in my own life.

Since childhood, church has been my second home, where worship healed my soul and fellowship gave me purpose. By my twenties, I was deeply involved in ministry: serving on the worship team, teaching Sunday school, and leading Bible studies. I loved God wholeheartedly and wanted nothing more than to serve Him with excellence.

But behind the smile, my life began to fracture.

It started with a phone call I will never forget. My mother's voice trembled as she told me my stepfather had been diagnosed with Stage IV cancer that had metastasized throughout his body. He had been my protector, my confidant, my rock. Watching one of the strongest men I knew grow weaker by the day broke something inside me.

Not long after, another blow came—one that would unravel me completely. I returned home from a medical mission trip to discover my then-husband's repeated infidelities. Betrayal layered itself on top of grief, and my world collapsed under the weight of compounded loss.

Still, no one at church knew.

I kept singing. I kept serving. I kept teaching about God's faithfulness while silently falling apart. Depression crept in slowly. Sleep became elusive. My appetite disappeared. Some days I could barely get out of bed, yet I forced myself to show up.

Why didn't I speak up?

Because somewhere along the way, I had been taught that strong Christians don't struggle with depression, that mental health challenges are spiritual weaknesses, and that joy and sorrow, faith and fear, are not allowed to coexist.

And so, I suffered in silence.

It wasn't until one quiet night, alone on my bedroom floor, that I poured out my heart in prayer. I started to ask God a barrage of questions: How could He love me and watch me go through so much pain without intervening? Does He even care about my pain? Does He even love me? Is He truly "Close to the broken hearted" like His Word says (Psalm 34:18)? How is it that in my deepest despair, He felt distant? How could He remain silent at such a time as this? After my slew of questions, I felt a sense of relief. A sense of peace overshadowed me.

My prayer turned from an audible wailing and lament to a whisper. I no longer demanded answers from God, and I simply asked that He see me. In that moment, the words from Matthew 12:20 came to my mind: "A bruised reed he will not break." That moment marked the beginning of honesty and the beginning of healing.

This book was born from that place.

I did not heal alone. I want to say that plainly because this book is about exactly that—the kind of care that actually heals.

I healed with the help of my pastor and his wife, who heard me, validated me, and supported me through the process. In a season when I was afraid that honesty would cost me community, they showed me that genuine pastoral care creates safety rather than taking it away.

I healed with the support of my friend Cinthia, who took me into her home for three months and asked for nothing in return. In my moment of despair, when I called her to get me, she arrived from thirty minutes away in less than ten. I still reflect on that with warmth, and now, with a great deal of humor. Her greatest gift was not her home, it was that she never once pressured me to hurry my healing or get over my losses. She simply stayed. She offered to take me to church with her, and I went. That small, unhurried invitation back to community was more powerful than she may ever know.

I healed with the help my friends Onyx, Jeta, Nikki, and Yayey, who refused to let depression have the last word. They took me to brunches, lunches, and dinners. Not to fix me, not to counsel me, but simply to share some laughter and remind me that life still had warmth in it.

What all these people had in common was their presence. They stayed. They did not judge, condemn, or shame me. They handled me with Christ-like compassion and grace. They attended to my physical, emotional, and spiritual needs. Not as a compulsory act, but as an expression of love.

These are examples of whole-person, Christ-driven care. A pastor and his wife who listened and validated. A friend who opened her home without condition. Friends who showed up with laughter and refused to let isolation win. That is the kind of care this book is written to call the church toward. Not a program, but a posture. Not a strategy, but a way of staying.

In many churches, mental health remains a taboo subject, spoken of quietly, if at all. This silence has consequences. People suffer alone. Leaders burn out. Communities miss the call to bear one another's burdens. And the body of Christ fractures under the weight of pain that was never meant to be carried in secret.

Healing Without Shame is an invitation, to sufferers and leaders alike, to rediscover what it means to be the body of Christ in a world grappling with mental anguish. This is not a book of perfect answers. It is a call to compassion, honesty, and courageous presence.

These pages will take you through the roots of stigma, the theology of whole-person care, the harm the church has sometimes caused and the repair it is capable of, the example of Jesus, and the practical work of becoming communities where no one suffers in silence. Some chapters will feel like permission. Some will feel like a mirror. A few may be difficult to read. All of them are written with you in mind.

Whoever you are, as you hold this book—whether you are hurting, leading, healing, or somewhere in between—I want you to know something before you turn the first page: You do not have to have it together to be here. This book was written in my bed of despair. It belongs to people who are still finding their way.

My prayer is that by the time you reach the final page, you will feel not only seen and supported, but freed—freed from the weight of hiding, freed toward the kind of honest, whole-person healing that God always intended, and freed into community with others who are learning, as you are, to heal without shame.

HOW TO USE THIS BOOK

This book was written to be read slowly.

It covers territory that many of us have been trained, consciously or not, to move past quickly—mental health, shame, spiritual harm, and the long and nonlinear work of healing. Some chapters may bring things to the surface that have been buried for a long time. If that happens, please be gentle with yourself. Set the book down when you need to. Come back when you are ready. There is no right pace.

Each chapter closes with a set of reflection questions. These are not tests or assignments. They are invitations—to slow down, to sit with what you have read, and to let it connect with your own life, your own community, and your own sense of what needs to change. Use them however serves you best. Write in a journal. Talk through them with a trusted friend. Sit with one question for a week. Or simply read them and let them work quietly in the background.

Below are a few thoughts on how different readers might approach this book.

IF YOU ARE PERSONALLY STRUGGLING

This book was written with you at the center. You do not need to read it as a resource to share with others or as a manual for fixing your church. You are allowed to read it for yourself. Read at your own pace. Skip sections that feel like too much right now and return to them later. If a chapter opens something tender, consider bringing it to a therapist, a trusted pastor, or a safe person in your life.

The reflection questions at the end of each chapter can serve as a gentle way to process what you have read before moving on. If a question feels too big, you are not obligated to answer it. Notice which ones you want to avoid. Sometimes those are the ones that matter most.

IF YOU ARE A PASTOR
OR MINISTRY LEADER

You are probably reading this with two people in mind: yourself, and the people in your care. I would encourage you to attend to yourself first. The questions about stigma, silence, and the cost of performing wellness are not only for your congregation. They are for you too. Leaders who have not done their own internal work on these themes can unintentionally perpetuate the very patterns this book addresses.

Chapters 5, 7, 8, and 9 are written with leaders directly in mind and offer practical frameworks for building healthier cultures of care. The reflection questions in these specific chapters are written through a leadership lens that you may find especially useful.

IF YOU ARE READING IN A
SMALL GROUP OR COMMUNITY

This book works well as a group study for church small groups, pastoral teams, seminary cohorts, counseling staff, or any community of people committed to doing this work together. The reflection questions at the end of each chapter include questions designed for group conversation.

A few suggestions for group use:

- Read the chapter individually before gathering.

- Choose two or three questions to discuss rather than trying to cover all five.

- Create a norm of confidentiality so people feel safe sharing honestly.

- Move slowly; one chapter per gathering is usually more fruitful than rushing.

Pay attention to the person in your group who is quiet. That person may be carrying the most.

IF YOU ARE A CAREGIVER,
COUNSELOR, OR THERAPIST

You will find both clinical and pastoral language in these pages, and that is intentional. This book lives in the space where the two traditions meet. The clinical concepts are presented accessibly—not because they are oversimplified, but because they are translated for a faith audience that may not have had prior exposure to trauma-informed frameworks.

The reflection questions may be useful as prompts for clients who are navigating the intersection of faith and mental health, or as discussion starters in training or supervision contexts. The References section at the back of the book points toward the deeper sources behind the frameworks explored here.

However you are reading this book, and whoever you are as you begin, you are welcome here. Exactly as you are.

BREAKING THE SILENCE

CHAPTER 1

THE STIGMA WITHIN

*Shame corrodes the very part of us
that believes we are capable of change.*

BRENÉ BROWN, *The Gifts of Imperfection*

I f you are reading this while carrying pain you have not felt safe naming or discussing in church, let me be the first to say it:

You are not weak.

You are not failing God.

You are not broken beyond repair.

Many people who love Jesus are quietly living with anxiety, depression, trauma, or emotional exhaustion. They pray. They serve. They show up. And when the pain does not get better, they often turn inward, wondering what they are doing wrong.

For some, the hardest part of mental health suffering is not the symptoms themselves. It is the shame that follows. When emotional distress is framed, explicitly or implicitly, as a spiritual problem, suffering becomes something to hide. People remain silent to avoid being condemned.

This is how stigma forms inside the church—not always through malice, but through misunderstanding. And misunderstanding, when left unaddressed, becomes culture.

The word *stigma* comes from the Greek word for a mark or brand— something pressed into the skin to identify a person as different, lesser, or outside the bounds of full belonging. In the social sciences, stigma describes the process by which a person is reduced from a full, complex human being to a single, diminished characteristic. Erving Goffman, whose foundational work on stigma has shaped decades of research, described it as a "spoiled identity"—the experience of being marked in a way that separates a person from those who are considered whole. When stigma attaches itself to mental health, the mark reads something like this: You are too broken, too weak, or too faithless to fully belong here. That is the wound beneath the wound—and it is the wound this book is written to address.

HOW STIGMA TAKES ROOT

Mental health stigma in faith communities rarely announces itself openly. More often, it appears in familiar phrases and unspoken expectations:

"Just trust God."

"Have you prayed about it?"

"Just speak life."

"Don't claim that diagnosis."

These responses are often well-intentioned. But for someone already struggling, they can feel dismissive. When pain is minimized ("it's not that bad") or spiritualized ("just pray about it"), that person's nervous system does not calm down. It tightens up and shifts into survival mode.

Over time, people learn an unspoken rule: This is not a safe place to be fully honest. So, they manage appearances, pretending to be fine. They soften their language. They spiritualize their symptoms. They stay silent.

THE COST OF SILENCE

Silence carries a heavy cost. When people are made to feel they must be silent,

- they stop asking for help;

- they isolate;

- they internalize guilt; and

- they burn out or quietly disappear.

Many sitting in pews are carrying invisible wounds: childhood abuse, chronic stress, complicated grief, domestic violence, medical trauma, or racial trauma. Loving God does not make a person immune to these experiences. It makes them human. When pain feels spiritually unacceptable, it often becomes heavier to carry.

When the church lacks language for emotional suffering, people can conclude that "God may accept me, but the church does not." Or worse, that "If the church doesn't accept this part of me, maybe God doesn't either." That is the hidden cost of silence.

If you are feeling discouraged because of your mental health struggles, let this sink in: God loves you in the midst of those struggles. His plans are not to harm you but to give you hope and a future.

> *"For I know the plans I have for you," declares*
> *the Lord, "plans to prosper you and not to harm*
> *you, plans to give you hope and a future."*
>
> **JEREMIAH 29:11**

Many believers cling to this verse as a promise of blessing, yet it is worth noting that it was spoken to a people living in exile—displaced, uncertain, and grieving. God's promise of hope was not given in comfort, but in captivity. This reminds us that mental and emotional suffering does not disqualify us from God's plans. We have hope even in our struggle, and God's purposes remain intact, even in our pain.

MENTAL HEALTH IS NOT
A SPIRITUAL FAILURE

Let me say this plainly: mental health struggles are not moral failures.

Depression is not laziness.

Anxiety is not a lack of faith.

Post-traumatic stress is not disobedience.

Needing medication is not a betrayal of God.

Seeking therapy does not diminish His authority.

Trauma reshapes our nervous system. Chronic stress alters our body. Depression affects our energy, cognition, and motivation at a biological level. These are physiological realities, not spiritual shortcomings.

Scripture reflects this truth. In 1 Kings 19, after a powerful spiritual victory, Elijah collapsed into despair and asked God to take his life. God did not rebuke him. God fed him, let him rest, and stayed nearby. God did not question Elijah's faith. He tended to his body and soul. That is compassionate, whole-person care.

If God responds to despair with nourishment and rest, the church must respond with the same wisdom.

WHAT THE WOUNDED NEED MOST

For those who are suffering, healing does not begin with answers. It begins with safety. What people need from the church is not perfection, but presence:

- To be believed

- To be listened to without correction

- To be met with curiosity instead of conclusions

- To be supported without being rushed

- To be allowed to heal at their own pace

Healing is not linear. Worship does not override trauma memory. Faith does not bypass the nervous system. God works with our humanity, not against it.

A WORD TO THE CHURCH

This chapter is addressed to the church as much as to those suffering within it, because stigma is not only a personal struggle but a communal one. It is formed in communities, and it must be dismantled in communities.

The church does not need to become a mental health clinic. But it is called to become a place where people feel emotionally safe enough to tell the truth, to ask for help, to be known without penalty. That kind of safety is not built through statements. It is built through what actually happens when someone finally says, "I am not okay."

A compassionate church learns to understand that behavior often communicates pain before words do. That listening matters more than fixing. That simplistic responses, however well-meaning, can cause harm when suffering is complex. That referring someone to professional care is an act of wisdom, not an admission of defeat. And that staying, simply remaining present when there are no answers, is often the most healing thing a community can offer.

The church fosters healing not by having all the answers, but by being willing to remain present when answers are unclear. Not by rushing people toward restoration, but by walking with them through the seasons of pain that precede it. That is not a clinical skill. It is a human one. And it is one the church has always been capable of, when it chooses to be.

WHERE HEALING BEGINS

Stigma loses its power when suffering is named without judgment or shame.

When churches say, "You are safe here. You don't have to hide."

When leaders say, "Faith includes struggle."

When communities say, "We will stay."

This is where restoration begins and where healing without shame becomes possible. Not in the absence of pain, but in the presence of people who refuse to look away from it.

I know the weight of stigma personally. I carried it while leading worship, while teaching Scripture, while smiling through services and quietly disappearing on the inside. I know what it costs to perform wellness you do not have. And I know because I lived through the other side of what it feels like when someone finally sees you and does not turn away.

This book is not theoretical. It was born from a season of despair. And if you find yourself in these pages, if you recognize your own silence, your own smile-through-it posture, your own private unraveling, know that you are not alone. You were never meant to carry this alone.

Healing begins with honesty.

Honesty requires safety.

And safety, for those of us who have not had it, requires the courage to believe it might be possible.

In the next chapter, we will explore why the suffering you carry is not a spiritual failure but a human experience that God, who formed us body and soul and spirit, understands completely.

REFLECTION QUESTIONS

1. Have you ever felt pressure to hide a mental health struggle in a church setting? What did that silence cost you?

2. What phrases or responses have you heard or offered that unintentionally communicated that someone's pain was unwelcome? What would a more compassionate response have looked like?

3. This chapter describes stigma forming through misunderstanding rather than malice. How does that framing change the way you think about addressing it in your community?

4. Where in your own life do you most need to hear the words "You are not weak. You are not failing God. You are not broken beyond repair"?

5. What is one specific way you could help create a safer space for honesty in your church, small group, or relationships this week?

CHAPTER 2

FAITH, TRAUMA, AND THE MIND

*God created us as body, soul, and spirit—
and healing that ignores any of these
three dimensions is incomplete.*

DIANE LANGBERG, *Suffering and the Heart of God*

For many Christians, seeking help for mental health feels like crossing an invisible boundary. One where faith is questioned.

You may have wondered, *If God heals, why do I still hurt? If prayer works, why do I need therapy? If I trust God, shouldn't this be easier?*

These questions are not signs of weak faith.

They are signs of honesty.

And the good news is this: Scripture has always told the truth about those questions. Long before the language of psychology existed, the Bible was already naming what you are feeling.

THE BIBLE TELLS THE
TRUTH ABOUT EMOTIONAL PAIN

One of the most damaging myths in the church is the belief that emotional suffering contradicts faith. Scripture tells a far more honest story.

David wrote psalms filled with despair, fear, anger, and grief.

Job questioned God openly amid unbearable loss.

Jeremiah wept publicly and repeatedly.

Elijah collapsed into suicidal despair.

Hannah wept so bitterly in her anguish that she was mistaken for being drunk.

Hagar, abandoned and alone in the wilderness with her dying child, cried out.

Jesus experienced anguish so intense that He sweat blood in Gethsemane.

None of these responses were condemned by God. Instead, God stayed present. The Bible does not shame emotional pain. It records it faithfully. Distress is not evidence of spiritual failure; it is evidence of humanity.

YOU ARE NOT ONLY
SPIRITUAL, YOU ARE HUMAN

Scripture presents human beings as integrated and whole. We are body, soul, and spirit—woven together, not compartmentalized. What affects one part of us affects the others.

Genesis 2:7 offers a foundational picture of what it means to be human:

> *"Then the Lord God formed man from the dust of*
> *the ground and breathed into his nostrils the breath*
> *of life, and the man became a living being."*

God formed the body from dust—physical, biological, embodied. Then He breathed into that body the breath of life—spirit. The result was not two separate parts, but a living being, an integrated soul.

Human beings are tripartite by design. The body includes the nervous system, brain chemistry, and physiological responses to stress. The soul encompasses our emotions, thoughts, memories, and internal experiences. The spirit is the part of us that communes with God.

Trauma and mental health struggles often affect the body and the soul. The nervous system can become dysregulated. Emotions can feel overwhelming or we feel numb. Our thought patterns can become distorted by fear or shame. These are not signs of spiritual weakness; they are signs that the body and soul have absorbed painful experiences.

When we address emotional wounds solely through spiritual intervention—prayer alone, Scripture alone, discipline alone—we unintentionally minimize the fullness of the person God designed. We reduce a complex, divinely integrated human being to a single dimension.

To ignore the body is to ignore God's formation from the dust.

To ignore the soul is to ignore the lived reality of being human.

To focus only on the spirit is to overlook the masterpiece God declared "very good" (Genesis 1:31).

You are not only a spirit in need of prayer.

You are a body that may need care.

You are a soul that may need support.

Trauma does not live only in memory. It lives in the nervous system.

Depression is not simply sadness. It is often exhaustion at a biological level.

Anxiety is not a failure to trust God. It is a body stuck in survival mode.

When churches address emotional suffering using spiritual language alone, people are left trying to heal neurological and emotional wounds without the tools they need. This gap often leads to shame, confusion, and a deep sense of spiritual inadequacy.

Healing becomes sustainable when the body is regulated, the soul is supported, and the spirit is nurtured.

THE QUESTION THAT CHANGES EVERYTHING

I want to share something that shifted how I saw nearly every person who walked into my office, and eventually how I understood my own story. It is simple: Painful experiences do not simply disappear when they are over. They settle into the body. They shape how a person responds to stress long after the original wound has healed. They influence whether the world feels safe or threatening in ways that are automatic, below the level of conscious choice.

When I began to understand this, the person who seemed dramatic became someone whose nervous system was doing exactly what it learned to do to stay safe. The person who kept pulling away from community stopped looking rebellious and started looking like they were seeking self-preservation. The person who shut down when someone raised their voice was not being difficult. They were surviving—the way the body learns to survive when it has been hurt before.

And this is where one of the most important shifts a church community can make lives—not in programs or policies, but in a single question. The difference between asking someone, "What is wrong with you?" and asking, "What happened to you?" is not merely semantic. It is the difference between threat and safety. Between shame and dignity. Between a person feeling like a problem to be managed and a person feeling like a human worth knowing.

When a church asks, "What happened to you?"—genuinely, without rushing toward a resolution—people feel something they may have been waiting years to feel: I am safe here. My story is worth telling.

I am not the problem. That question, asked with patience and without an agenda, can be the beginning of someone's healing. I have watched it happen. I have experienced it myself.

WHEN THE BODY REMEMBERS WHAT THE MIND HAS TRIED TO FORGET

I will never forget July 4, 1996.

I had been in the United States for only six months. The newness of everything still felt fragile—a new country, a new way of living, a new kind of quiet I was still learning to trust. I was sitting in the living room, watching television, when without warning the night outside erupted in what sounded exactly like gunshots and missiles.

I did not think. I did not reason. I moved.

I threw myself off the couch and pressed my body behind it, heart pounding, every nerve alive with a terror I recognized from somewhere deep and old. In that moment, I was that child again—small, terrified, and dodging bullets in Liberia.

It was fireworks.

July 4th. American Independence Day. The country was celebrating its freedom with light and noise, and my body had received every burst as a threat.

I had crossed borders, changed continents, and started a new life. But the body does not consult the mind before it responds. The body simply remembers. And that night in the living room, every fiber of mine remembered with absolute clarity what my mind had tried so hard to forget.

When someone is in the grip of a trauma response, their brain is not choosing fear. It is responding automatically, trying to protect a person who was once in danger. In those moments, telling someone to "just trust God" or "choose joy" is not addressing what is actually happening. The issue is not belief. It is biology. And addressing it requires more than spiritual encouragement, however sincere. It requires the kind of whole-person care that honors the body, the soul, and the spirit together, including therapy and sometimes medication, not as replacements for faith, but as expressions of God's provision through wisdom and science.

THERAPY IS NOT A LACK OF FAITH

One of the most harmful beliefs in Christian culture is that needing therapy means prayer was insufficient or that faith was lacking. Interestingly, we do not apply this logic to physical health.

We do not shame insulin.

We do not spiritualize broken bones.

We do not condemn surgery.

Yet we shame, spiritualize, and condemn the need for mental health care. Mental health care is health care. Therapy helps people make sense of their pain, process trauma safely, learn emotional regulation, heal attachment wounds, and rebuild trust and stability. Medication can help stabilize brain chemistry so deeper healing work becomes possible.

None of this diminishes God's power.

It reflects God's provision.

FAITH AND PSYCHOLOGY BELONG TOGETHER

For too long, faith and psychology have been framed as competitors: one spiritual, one scientific; one sacred, one secular. But this division is false, and it has cost the church dearly. Trauma-informed theology begins by affirming this truth: faith and psychology are not opposing forces. They are complementary ways of understanding the whole person whom God made and loves.

As both a psychologist and a woman of faith, I find the integration of psychology and faith deeply meaningful. When held together well, they honor the whole person (body, soul, spirit) just as God designed.

Psychology helps us understand why we hurt. Faith holds our spirit intact while we heal.

Psychology says, "Your story makes sense given what you've lived through." Faith says, "Your story is not over."

Psychology reduces shame by normalizing survival responses. Faith replaces condemnation with grace.

A trauma-informed church understands that prayer and therapy work best together, that faith supports healing without rushing it, that God works through people, process, and science, and that presence often heals more than answers.

When the church becomes a bridge instead of a barrier, people are more likely to seek help early: before crisis, before isolation, before collapse.

WHERE THE CHURCH HAS STRUGGLED

When churches frame mental health struggles as a lack of faith, a sin issue, a spiritual attack, or emotional immaturity, they often deepen harm without intending to. When we misunderstand our design, we misdiagnose our misery. If we believe human beings are primarily spiritual, we will only offer spiritual solutions. But when we remember that we are body, soul, and spirit, our response becomes more compassionate and more comprehensive.

I once knew a young woman who suffered for years from debilitating migraines. The pain was so severe it disrupted her work, sleep, and daily functioning. Over time, the chronic physical suffering gave way to something even heavier: deep depression. She began to feel hopeless, exhausted, and emotionally numb. Eventually, her despair escalated into thoughts of not wanting to live.

Afraid of where her mind was going, she did what many churches teach people to do. She reached out. She told her pastor. She confided in church leaders. She explained both the physical agony and the emotional weight that followed.

But instead of receiving holistic care, her suffering was reduced to a spiritual problem. She was encouraged to pray more. She was told to trust God for healing. She was reminded that faith requires perseverance. No one asked about the severity of her migraines. No one suggested she see a neurologist. No one assessed the seriousness of her depression. No one recommended therapy.

Her symptoms were spiritualized. Her emotional suffering was unintentionally minimized. This is what overspiritualization can do. It compresses complex human experiences into singular spiritual explanations. It assumes that if faith increases, suffering will decrease. But migraines can have neurological causes. Depression can have biological, psychological, and environmental components. Suicidal ideation can signal overwhelming distress rather than weak belief.

What she needed was not more faith. She needed integrated care. Prayer and medical evaluation, spiritual encouragement and therapeutic support, compassion and a referral.

Eventually, she sought professional help on her own. A neurologist helped her manage the migraines. Therapy helped her untangle the depression that had quietly taken root. Her faith did not collapse. It deepened—not because she was told to try harder, but because her humanity was finally honored.

Faith did not replace treatment.
Faith walked alongside it.

This is the integration the church is invited to learn. Healthy churches normalize mental health care, encourage professional support without shame, allow healing to unfold slowly, and pray *with* people—not *over* them.

A WORD TO THOSE
WHO ARE STILL HURTING

If you are still struggling after praying, believing, serving, and hoping, hear this clearly:

You have not failed God.

God has not abandoned you.

Your need for help is not a spiritual deficiency.

Healing is not about becoming stronger.

It is about becoming safer.

As a psychologist and as a person of faith, I have lived on both sides of this truth. I have sat with people whose suffering had been spiritualized for so long that they had begun to believe the problem was their faith. They thought that if they just believed harder, prayed longer, trusted more completely, the pain would finally lift. And I have sat with those same people on the other side of integrated care—when both the spiritual and the clinical were honored together—and watched something in them soften and open that no amount of spiritual pressure alone had been able to reach.

God is not threatened by your need for help. He is not keeping score of how many times you have cried out without receiving the answer you asked for. He designed your nervous system. He understands the biology of your suffering. And He meets you in it—through prayer, yes, and also through the therapist who helps you find language for what happened to you, and the doctor who helps stabilize what your body can no longer regulate on its own.

> *"Whoever dwells in the shelter of the*
> *Most High will rest in the shadow of the Almighty….*
> *'He is my refuge and my fortress.'"*
>
> **PSALM 91:1-2**

That shelter is not only a spiritual location. It is the lived experience of safety in God's presence, in trustworthy community, in the care of those equipped to help you heal. In the next chapter, we will gently explore what happens when the church responds poorly to that need and how listening, humility, and repair can begin to restore trust where harm has occurred.

REFLECTION QUESTIONS

1. Have you ever experienced the false divide between faith and mental health, the sense that seeking help was somehow a failure of trust in God? Where did that belief come from, and how has it shaped your choices?

2. The chapter describes human beings as body, soul, and spirit, with all three needing care. Which dimension do you find your church most attends to? Which is most neglected?

3. What does the story of the young woman with migraines reveal about the cost of offering only spiritual responses to complex human suffering? Have you witnessed something similar?

4. How do you respond to the statement, "Medication and therapy are not a failure of faith. They are an expression of God's provision"? What resistance, if any, do you notice in yourself?

5. What would integrated care, prayer and professional support working together look like in your community? What would need to change to make that possible?

CHAPTER 3

WHEN THE CHURCH CAUSES HARM

*The opposite of belonging is fitting in. Fitting in is
assessing a situation and becoming who you need to
be to be accepted. Belonging does not require us to
change who we are; it requires us to be who we are.*

BRENÉ BROWN, *The Gifts of Imperfection*

For many people, the most painful part of their mental health journey was not the anxiety, depression, or trauma itself. It was how the church responded to it.

If you reached out for help and were dismissed, corrected, or quietly avoided, your pain is real. And it deserves to be named.

I want to begin this chapter, not with a framework or a list, but with a confession. Writing it has been one of the hardest things I have done. Not because the truth is difficult to know, but because it is difficult to hold. I love the church. I was formed by the church. I have given my life to the church. And I have watched the church, with good intentions and genuine love, cause profound harm to people who came to it bleeding.

That grief does not have a clean resolution. I am not sure it should.

Over the years, I have had the humbling and often heartbreaking experience of sitting with people whose wounds were deepened not by the world, but by the community they trusted most. I have listened to their stories as a psychologist. I have prayed with them as a minister. And I have learned that the two roles are not as separate as we sometimes pretend. The soul does not separate its suffering into neat categories of spiritual and clinical. It simply hurts. And it needs someone to stay.

Some were told to pray harder.

Some were told they lacked faith.

Some were offered Scripture instead of support.

Some were labeled "negative," or "too much."

And many learned, often painfully, that church did not feel like a safe place to be honest.

THE WOUND BENEATH THE WOUND

There is a kind of injury that does not come from the original pain. It comes from the response to it. When someone finally finds the courage to name what they are carrying—the depression they have hidden for years, the anxiety that wakes them before dawn, the grief that has not lifted—and they are met with dismissal or correction, something breaks that is very difficult to repair. They came exposed and vulnerable. They took the risk of being known. And the message they received, however unintentionally, was that this is not the right kind of suffering.

That injury, the wound beneath the wound (or secondary trauma), can cut deeper than the original pain. It teaches a lesson that is hard to unlearn: It is not safe to be seen here. The consequences are far-reaching. People withdraw. They isolate. They carry their pain alone and in secret. And some, as I will share in a moment, carry it until they can carry it no longer.

People do not leave the church because they are fragile.

They leave because they are wounded.

And sometimes, they do not leave at all. They stay hollowed out, pretending to be fine, and singing songs about freedom while suffering in silence.

WHEN WORDS MEANT TO HELP DO HARM

One of the most common ways the church unintentionally hurts those who are struggling is through spiritual bypassing or using the language of faith to move past emotional pain rather than entering it. It sounds like:

- "God won't give you more than you can bear."

- "Just speak life over your situation."

- "You need to claim your victory."

- "Don't receive that diagnosis."

- "This is a spiritual issue, not a mental one."

The people who say these things usually love the person they are telling them to. They are not trying to harm. But for someone already drowning in shame, these phrases can feel less like a lifeline and more like a weight. They communicate something the speaker never intended: Your pain makes me uncomfortable. I don't know how to stay with you in this.

Spiritual bypassing does not heal trauma. It suppresses it. And suppressed pain does not disappear; it finds another way to surface.

I think of a mother I know who lost her son to gun violence. Her grief was raw, consuming, and entirely reasonable. She had lost a child. And yet, when she brought that grief into her church community, she was not met with presence but with redirection. She was told she should not mourn because her son was with the Lord and that was reason for rejoicing. Someone quoted Scripture at her, that we are to rejoice in all seasons because it is the will of God. Another person, meaning well, reminded her that it could be worse, that some people had lost their entire families to war, fire, and natural disasters, and at least she still had two other living children.

She told me later that she left that conversation feeling more alone than she had felt standing at her son's graveside. The people around her loved her. She knew that. But love without the capacity to sit with grief is not enough. And grief that cannot be named in the community of faith does not disappear. It goes underground, into the body, into isolation, into a slow and quiet withdrawal from everything that was once a source of life.

This is what spiritual bypassing costs. Not only a moment of comfort withheld, but a person's trust that the church is a place where the full weight of human experience is welcome.

Jesus never bypassed pain.

He acknowledged it.

He entered it.

He stayed.

If we are to reflect Him, we must do the same.

A STORY I HAVE NEVER FORGOTTEN

I want to tell you about someone I knew. I will protect his identity, as I always do, but I cannot protect you from the weight of his story. And I do not think I should, because his story is the reason this chapter must be written honestly.

He was a young minister, faithful, gifted, deeply loved by his congregation. He grew up in the church. Faith was not abstract to him;

it was real, the foundation of everything he understood about who he was and why he was here. He loved the Lord with a sincerity that was evident to everyone around him.

He also lived with depression.

Not the kind that announces itself loudly, but the quiet kind. The kind that hides behind a sermon well-preached, a smile held steady through a Sunday service, a life of service offered generously while the inner world grows darker and more silent. He served faithfully. He showed up. He poured himself out for others. And privately, in the spaces no one saw, he was struggling to survive.

He did what we hope people will do. He reached out. He told those closest to him—people of deep faith who loved him genuinely—what he was experiencing. He told the leaders of his church. He asked for help. And he was told, gently but clearly, that what he was experiencing was a spiritual battle. The answer was to pray more, to fast more, to trust God more deeply. The people around him loved him. I believe that with my whole heart. But they did not have the language for what he was carrying.

I walked with him for a season. I encouraged him to seek help from a mental health professional. I reminded him that doing so was not a failure of faith, but an act of stewardship. God, who formed us body and soul, also works through doctors, therapists, and healers. Asking for help was not a betrayal of his calling, but an expression of it. He listened. He said he would seek help.

But the stigma spoke louder than the encouragement.

He died by suicide when his pain became too unbearable to carry alone.

I have held his story for years. I hold it still. And I share it now carefully, tenderly, with the full weight of the grief it deserves. Because I believe that there is someone who is reading this book that is where he was. Someone who is faithful and gifted and loved, yet privately, silently, disappearing. And I need that person to know that your pain is real. Your life is precious. And the church, at its best, is not a place that will hand you Scripture and turn away. It is a place that will stay.

If you are that person, please reach out to a mental health professional. Not because your faith is insufficient, but because you are worth the care. And to the church: we must do better. Not out of guilt, but out of love, because people like him are sitting in our pews every Sunday, waiting to find out whether it is safe to tell the truth.

He is not the only one.

I think of a woman who came to me after years of enduring physical, emotional, financial, and sexual abuse at the hands of her husband. She had found the courage to bring this to her pastor. What she received was not protection or support; she was told to stay and that God hates divorce. That her body belonged to her husband. That this was her cross to bear. That if she kept praying and believing, God could restore the marriage and change her husband.

She told me that the conversation with her pastor left her more wounded than the abuse itself because she had come to God's representative in her most vulnerable moment and had been sent back into harm. She stopped going to church. She began to question God's love for her. She wondered whether the God she had worshipped for years saw her suffering and simply did not care.

She eventually found the courage to leave her husband. She stayed away from church for almost ten years. She is now happily married with two children and has found a church community that supports her—all of her. Her story did not end in the pastor's office. But the ten years it cost her to find her way back were shaped, in no small part, by a response that used Scripture to protect a harmful marriage rather than a vulnerable woman.

There is also the story of a worship leader, gifted, faithful, and deeply committed to her community. She had been told by her women's pastor and mentor that she could trust her with anything, that she would be a support and a safe presence. Believing that, she shared something deeply personal—her struggle with her sexuality. It was an act of enormous courage and vulnerability.

The Sunday after that conversation, that pastor preached about the lady's story from the pulpit.

She left the church and never returned. She began to resent God, believing He was as cruel and untrustworthy as the leaders who had represented Him. The wound was not only the betrayal of confidence. It was the theological message her community had sent without words. A message that said, you are not safe here. Your honesty is a weapon that will be used against you.

It was not until she began to process her hurt in therapy that she was able to do something she had not been able to do on her own: separate the way the church had treated her from the way God treats her. She is still not attending church. But she is working on her relationship with God at her own pace, praying, reading Scripture, engaging with devotional material, and occasionally watching online sermons that speak to her spirit. Healing, for her, looks like this for now. And that is enough.

WHEN LEADERS ARE HURTING, TOO

Here is something the church rarely speaks about. The loneliness of those who lead. Church leaders are not immune to mental health struggles. In many ways, they are more vulnerable, carrying the weight of others' pain while rarely having a safe space to name their own. The culture of ministry often demands that leaders appear strong, remain hopeful, have answers, and never need help. But that expectation is not from God. It is from a culture that has confused performance with faithfulness.

Remember the young minister I told you about earlier? He was not weak. He was human. And the humanity that made him compassionate, that made him gifted, needed tending. When leaders are given permission to be human (to rest, to struggle, to seek care) they create cultures where those they serve feel the same permission.

Care must extend to those who carry responsibility, not only to those who sit in the pews.

NAMING HARM WITHOUT CONDEMNATION

This chapter is not about blaming the church. It is about telling the truth so healing can begin.

The church has, at times, misunderstood mental illness, overspiritualized suffering, minimized trauma, failed to listen well, and caused harm it never intended to cause. These are not the actions of malicious people. They are the actions of people who were never given the tools to respond differently.

Acknowledging this is not an attack on faith.

It is an act of honesty.

And honesty, the kind that does not flinch from what is true, is where healing begins.

The church I believe in is not too fragile for this conversation. It is exactly strong enough to have it.

WHAT REPAIR ACTUALLY REQUIRES

If there has been harm, and there has been for many reading this, repair is possible. But it cannot be rushed and it cannot be performed. It must be embodied, slowly and consistently, in the way a community chooses to show up.

For trust to be rebuilt, the church must learn to:

- Listen without correcting.

- Believe people's stories, even when it is uncomfortable.

- Apologize when harm has occurred, without defense or justification.

- Stop rushing people toward resolution they are not ready for.

- Create safety before offering guidance.

Repair is not a moment. It is a posture. It is a daily, ongoing choice to remain present with people in their pain. Healing trust takes time, and it should. Trust that is rebuilt slowly is trust that lasts.

A WORD TO THOSE WHO HAVE BEEN HURT

If you were harmed by a careless response, if you were dismissed or corrected or made to feel that your suffering was a spiritual problem rather than a human one, I want to say something directly to you:

You are not imagining it.

You are not too sensitive.

You are not holding a grudge.

You are not wrong for pulling away to protect yourself.

God does not require you to return to unsafe spaces to prove your devotion. He does not ask you to absorb harm quietly in the name of grace.

Distance can be an act of wisdom.

Boundaries can be holy.

Grieve what was lost. Give yourself permission to heal at your own pace. And know that the God who sees you is not standing at a distance, arms crossed, waiting for you to recover faster.

He is right here.

Closer than your next breath.

And He is not afraid of what you are carrying.

A GENTLE INVITATION FORWARD

Some reading this will feel torn, longing for community, yet deeply afraid of being hurt again. That tension is not a sign of weakness. It is a sign of wisdom earned the hard way. I am not asking you to rush back. I am only asking you to stay open to the possibility that some communities are learning, that some leaders are growing, that the church at its truest is still capable of becoming what it was always meant to be.

Healing does not require urgency; it requires safety.

And safety, when it is finally found, is worth every careful, unhurried step it took to get there.

In the next chapter, we will turn toward Jesus. Not as a theological concept, but as a living model of what safe presence looks like.

REFLECTION QUESTIONS

1. Has the church ever caused you harm in the context of mental health? If so, what would you have needed from that community that it did not offer?

2. This chapter introduces the concept of "secondary wounding" or harm caused not by the original pain, but by how others respond to it. Have you experienced or witnessed this? What did it look like?

3. How does your church or community currently respond when a leader is struggling? What norms, spoken or unspoken, shape that response?

4. This chapter says that naming harm is not an attack on faith; it is an act of repentance. How do you hold those two things together? Does that framing change how you think about accountability in the church?

5. What would genuine repair look like in a church community that has caused harm? What would you need to see, over time, to begin to trust again?

PART II

THE WAY OF
COMPASSION

CHAPTER 4

JESUS, THE WOUNDED, AND THE WAY OF COMPASSION

*Jesus never asked the wounded to compose
themselves before He drew near. He moved
toward suffering, not away from it.*

If the last chapter was difficult to read, I understand.

Naming the ways the church has caused harm is not a light thing. It can stir up old grief, the memory of a conversation where you felt dismissed, a leader who looked away, a community that kept singing while you were quietly falling apart. If you arrived at this chapter carrying some of that, please know that you are allowed to carry it here. You do not have to set it down to keep reading.

I want to bring you somewhere that I return to often, especially in the seasons when ministry has been heavy, when I have sat with suffering I could not fix, when the gap between the church as it is and the church as it ought to be has felt unbearably wide.

I bring you to Jesus. Not to a theological argument, not to a doctrinal summary, but to the actual moments in the gospels when He encountered real people in real pain, and what He did when He found them.

Because if you have been hurt by the church, you may have also, somewhere along the way, begun to wonder about God—whether He too is distant, whether He too responds to suffering with disappointment or correction or silence. I want to gently address that question, not with a lecture, but with a portrait. Because the clearest picture we have of who God is, is not a doctrine. It is a person.

And that person, when He encountered the wounded, never once turned away.

HE WAS SAFE FOR THE HURTING

Something quietly remarkable runs through the gospel accounts, if you read them slowly enough. People who were suffering were drawn to Jesus. Not reluctantly, but with a kind of instinctive, urgent seeking. The grieving came to Him. The outcast came. The frightened, the ashamed, the ones who had been told for years that they were too broken to belong all found their way to Him through crowds, through darkness, through their own desperation.

When someone has been hurt, repeatedly dismissed, shamed, or made to feel unsafe, they become acutely attuned to their environment, constantly and often unconsciously reading the room: Is this place safe? Will I be accepted here? If I tell the truth, what will happen to me? They protect themselves. They wait. But they move, sometimes with astonishing courage, toward safety.

The fact that wounded people were drawn to Jesus tells us something essential about the kind of presence He carried. He was not a safe space because He announced Himself to be one. He was safe because of what actually happened when hurting people encountered Him.

He did not interrogate their pain.

He did not require them to compose themselves before He came close.

He did not shame them for their weakness or their fear.

He did not rush their healing to fit His schedule.

He slowed down.

He noticed.

He stayed.

If you have spent years in communities that moved too fast, that offered answers before they offered presence, I want you to sit with this. The Jesus of the gospels is not in a hurry with you. He is not waiting for you to become more manageable before He draws near. He is already near.

HE ASKED BEFORE HE ACTED

One of the things I love most about Jesus is how often He asked questions before acting. Not rhetorical questions. Not questions designed to make a point. Genuine, open, unhurried questions: What do you want me to do for you? Do you want to be made well? Why are you afraid?

These questions restore agency. They assume nothing. They honor consent. Trauma strips people of control over their bodies, emotions, and stories. Jesus returned that control. He did not treat people as projects. He treated them as participants in their own healing.

If you have experienced the church as a place that acted *on* you rather than *with* you, that offered answers to questions no one thought to ask, Jesus offers something quietly revolutionary. He waits to hear from you before He moves.

He is not here to project onto your pain.

He is not here to prescribe before He listens.

He is here, first, to ask.

HE WEPT

In John 11 Jesus arrives at the tomb of Lazarus. He knows resurrection is coming. He knows death will not have the final word. And yet, deeply moved with compassion, He weeps.

I have read this passage many times and it never ceases to amaze me that Jesus did not bypass the grief to get to the miracle. He did not say, "There is no need to cry, watch what I am about to do." He honored the sorrow. He entered it. He let it matter.

If you have been told you should be over something by now, if you have been hurried past your grief by people who meant well, I want you to picture this image: the Son of God, standing at the edge of loss, weeping. Not performing sorrow, but genuinely moved, genuinely present, genuinely unwilling to rush past what was real.

Faith does not cancel sorrow.

It holds it.

Your grief is not evidence of insufficient faith. It is evidence of love. And Jesus, who wept for His friend, is not unmoved by yours.

HE DID NOT SHAME THE SUFFERING

In Mark 5 there is a man living among the tombs—someone we would describe today as experiencing severe psychological distress. He had been isolated from his community, stripped of belonging, dispossessed of his identity, and lived in the place designated for the dead. He was the kind of person that communities tend to look away from. Too loud. Too much. Too frightening. Too far gone.

Jesus went to him. He crossed over to where this man was (in his isolation, in his anguish) and engaged him as a person. He asked his name. He restored his dignity. He gave him back his identity and his belonging.

To every person who has felt like the man among the tombs, exiled from community, unsure of whether you still belong anywhere, Jesus has already crossed over to where you are.

You are not too much.

You are not too far.

You have not wandered beyond the reach of His compassion.

Your identity and your belonging was never contingent on your stability. It was given to you before any of this began.

HE DID NOT DEMAND STRENGTH FROM THE WEAK

Nowhere in the gospels does Jesus say, "Get yourself together first, then come to me." Nowhere does He say, "Come back when you are healed." He welcomed people as they were.

The woman who had been bleeding for twelve years reached out and touched the hem of His garment in a crowd. He stopped. He turned. He called her forward, not to correct her but to honor her (Mark 5:24-29). The father, whose son suffered, fell before Jesus crying, "I do believe; help me overcome my unbelief" (Mark 9:23-25). Jesus did not rebuke the doubt. He honored the honesty.

If you have been made to feel that your mental health struggles make you a burden to the church, that is not the message of Jesus. He is not burdened by your need. He is not waiting for you to be less complicated before He draws close.

He is already close.

He has always been close.

And He welcomes you, right now, exactly as you are,

with everything you are carrying.

WHAT THIS REVEALS ABOUT GOD

I have walked with many people for whom the image of God became distorted, not by the Bible, but by how God was represented to them by people who carried authority in their lives. A God who is never satisfied. A God who is disappointed in your pace. A God who requires performance before He offers love.

If that is the God you are carrying, I understand why faith feels exhausting. But I want to invite you to look again at Jesus because He is, as the writer of Hebrews tells us, the exact representation of God's nature.

A God who draws near to the grieving.

A God who asks before He acts.

A God who weeps at the edges of loss.

A God who crosses over to the isolated.

A God who is gentle with the bruised, and patient with those barely holding on.

God is not disappointed in you.

God is not threatened by your questions.

God is not offended by your need.

He is the same yesterday, today, and forever—and who He was to the wounded people in the gospels, He is to you, right now, wherever you are as you read these words.

WHAT THIS MEANS FOR THE CHURCH

If the church is the body of Christ, the continuation of His presence in the world, then His posture must become ours. To be the church is to be the kind of community where suffering people feel the same pull toward safety that drew them to Jesus: to be the community that asks before it acts, that weeps with those who weep, that crosses over to the isolated, that welcomes the struggling without demanding they stabilize themselves first.

A church that reflects Jesus:

- Prioritizes safety over spectacle

- Chooses presence over performance

- Allows healing to be slow and nonlinear

- Honors emotion rather than policing it

- Makes room for silence, doubt, tears, and questions

Jesus did not build His ministry on image management.

He built it on love.

And love, the kind that enters suffering rather than bypassing it, is what we are called to embody.

A WORD TO THE WOUNDED READER

If your relationship with God has become complicated because of what the church did or failed to do, if the harm you experienced in His name has made Him feel distant or unsafe, I want to offer you something—not an argument and not a theological correction, but just this:

The Jesus of the gospels is not the one who hurt you. What was done in His name was done by imperfect, sometimes harmful, sometimes well-meaning but misguided people who did not fully understand the God they were trying to represent. Their failure is real. Your wound is real. And Jesus, who sees everything, is not asking you to minimize either one.

In the next chapter, we will explore what it looks like for a church to move from good intentions to genuine practice—

building the kind of culture where people actually experience the safety that Jesus modeled.

REFLECTION QUESTIONS

1. Which Gospel encounter with Jesus in this chapter stayed with you the most: the woman with the issue of blood, the man living in the tombs, or the raising of Lazarus? What does that particular story say to the part of you that is still healing?

2. This chapter says Jesus asked questions rather than assuming. Think of someone in your life who is struggling. What question could you ask them this week that would communicate genuine curiosity rather than a preformed conclusion?

3. How does the image of Jesus weeping at Lazarus's tomb, not as a failure of faith, but as an expression of love, change how you understand grief in your own life?

4. If Jesus is the model for how the church should respond to the wounded, what gaps do you see between that model and the current practice of your community?

5. Has your image of God ever been distorted by a painful religious experience? What would it mean for you to encounter Jesus as He is described in this chapter—gentle, unhurried, and unafraid of your pain?

CHAPTER 5

CREATING A CULTURE OF CARE

*People will forget what you said. People
will forget what you did. But people will
never forget how you made them feel.*

MAYA ANGELOU

Healing does not happen in environments where people feel rushed, judged, or invisible.

It happens in environments where there is safety, consistency, and compassion.

I have thought a great deal about what it really takes to create a church culture where people feel safe enough to tell the truth. Not safe in the abstract, not safe because the sign outside says "All Are Welcome," but genuinely, bodily, practically safe in the way that allows a person who has been hurt to slowly, carefully lower their guard.

The answer, in my experience, is never a single program or policy or sermon series. The answer is in a culture of care. Culture is not created by declarations. It is created by what happens in the room, in the conversation after the service, in the way a leader responds when someone finally says something vulnerable, and in the thousands of small moments that accumulate over time into either safety or its absence.

A church culture of care is not built through statements. It is built through practice and how leaders respond when someone says, "I'm not okay."

Do we correct first or listen?

Do we spiritualize quickly or ask deeper questions?

Do we offer prayer alone or prayer and practical support?

Culture is revealed in moments of vulnerability. And if the church is to reflect Christ faithfully, it must create environments where honesty is not punished, therapy is not stigmatized, and suffering is not spiritualized away.

> *"For we are God's handiwork,*
> *created in Christ Jesus to do good works."*
> **EPHESIANS 2:10**

The Greek word translated as "handiwork" is the word from which we get "poem." It carries a sense of artistry, of intentional, careful creation. If every person is crafted by God with that kind of intentional artistry, then mental health challenges do not erase the beauty of that work. They do not make someone defective or less than. A compassionate church learns to see people as sacred creations, not spiritual problems to solve.

A culture of care is not a program to be launched. It is a posture to be embodied. It is a way of being with one another in the presence of pain that eventually becomes simply the way the community is.

SAFETY IS THE FOUNDATION, NOT THE GOAL

Every person who has experienced trauma is, in some part of themselves, constantly reading the room. This is not a choice or a habit. It is a survival response. The nervous system's learned way of asking, before it does anything else, *Is it safe to be here? Is it safe to be honest? If I tell the truth, what will happen to me?*

This means that safety is not the destination a caring church works toward. It is the prerequisite for everything else. People cannot receive care they do not feel safe enough to access. They cannot be honest in environments where honesty has historically been met with correction or dismissal. They cannot heal in communities where they feel they must manage how they appear.

A caring church communicates safety not through slogans, but through consistent, repeated, trustworthy behavior: language that does not judge, leadership that responds with care rather than alarm, strict confidentiality around what is shared, boundaries that are clear and kept, and a genuine willingness to listen without immediately reaching for a solution.

Safety is not created by saying, "You're safe here."

It is created by what happens when someone finally tells the truth.

And then by what happens the next time.

And the time after that.

THE WORDS WE USE
SHAPE THE WORLD WE CREATE

Language matters more than most of us realize. The words spoken in a church (from the pulpit, in small groups, in one-on-one conversations) form the emotional architecture of that community. They tell people what is safe to feel, what is acceptable to name, what kind of suffering will be welcomed, and what kind will need to be kept quiet.

I have watched the air go out of a room when a well-meaning leader responded to someone's disclosed struggle with "Others have it worse," or "God won't give you more than you can bear," or the particularly damaging "You just need to let it go." The person who had gathered the courage to speak did not say anything more. They nodded. They smiled. And they did not speak about it again.

These phrases are usually offered with genuine care, but they communicate something below the surface that their speakers never intend: Your pain is not acceptable. Your pain is inconvenient. We don't have room for it here. Please find a way to be less difficult.

Trauma-informed churches learn to notice this language and replace it with something different; something that communicates dignity and presence. They learn to say, "That sounds incredibly difficult. Thank you for trusting me with this. You don't have to go through this alone. How can I support you right now?" These phrases do something that the spiritual bypassing phrases cannot: They regulate the nervous system. They signal safety. They tell the body, as much as the mind, that this is a place where it is allowed to stop bracing.

This is not a minor or cosmetic change. It is a fundamental reorientation in how a community holds its most vulnerable members.

LEADERS SET THE EMOTIONAL TONE

There is something I have observed consistently across the communities I have worked with and served in: The emotional culture of a church almost always reflects the emotional culture of its leadership. Not the stated values, but the actual, lived, daily practice of how leaders respond to complexity, to failure, and to their own humanity.

When leaders are willing to acknowledge their own limitations and struggles, when they speak openly about seeking support, when they model rest without apology and boundaries without guilt, they give their congregation something more valuable than any program. They give them permission. Permission to be human. Permission to need help. Permission to be something other than fine.

I have seen this work in both directions. I have watched a leader's transparency about their own mental health journey open a floodgate of honesty in a community that had been carefully managing its image for years. And I have watched a leader's implicit demand for performed wellness (the unspoken rule that struggles should be resolved quickly and privately) create a culture where suffering went underground, where people smiled through services while quietly falling apart.

Vulnerability from leadership does not weaken authority. In my experience, it deepens trust in ways that competence and certainty alone cannot achieve. It reveals the humanity of leadership, making them more relatable and accessible to the people they lead.

CARE THAT IS SHARED CAN BE SUSTAINED

One of the most common ways well-intentioned churches create unsustainable care cultures is by centralizing everything. The pastor becomes the person everyone calls. The pastoral care team carries more than any small group of humans can hold. The caregiver who was gifted at being present gets consumed by a volume of need that depletes them entirely.

Care was never designed to work this way. The body of Christ, as Paul describes it, distributes responsibility across many members, each carrying what it was designed to carry, none carrying what belongs to the whole (1 Corinthians 12:12–27). A culture of care does not funnel everything toward a single point or person. It equips the entire community to notice, to listen, to offer practical support, to know when to refer, and to simply show up and stay.

This kind of distributed care does not happen by accident. It grows in communities that are intentional about equipping their people—not with clinical training, but with something simpler and equally powerful: the willingness to notice, to ask, to stay, and to say gently when the moment comes, "I think you need more support than I can offer, and I want to help you find it." When that capacity lives in many people rather than one, no single person has to carry what was always meant for the whole body.

PARTNERING WITH PROFESSIONALS IS AN ACT OF FAITHFULNESS

When I hear church leaders speak about mental health care as something that competes with faith, I understand the fear beneath it: the worry that psychology will crowd out prayer, that therapy will substitute for the Holy Spirit, that turning to a professional somehow signals a failure of trust in God. I have had that conversation more times than I can count. And each time, I want to say the same thing gently but directly: that fear is not from God. It comes from a misunderstanding of how God works—and the true width of His provision.

God heals through prayer and Scripture and community. He also heals through the neurologist who finally names what has been causing someone pain, through the therapist who helps a person find language for what happened to them, and through the psychiatrist who adjusts medication until someone can finally sleep. These are not competing paths. They are the same river, flowing from the same source, toward the same end.

You do not have to choose between
faith and care. You can do both.

Healthy churches build formal and informal relationships with trusted mental health professionals. They maintain referral lists. They speak about therapy and medication from the pulpit without shame. They make it as natural to recommend a counselor as to recommend a doctor. And in doing so, they remove one of the most significant barriers between suffering people and the help they need: the sense that choosing clinical care means choosing against God.

MAKING ROOM FOR LAMENT

There is a form of spiritual harm that is rarely named but widely felt—the harm of being in a community that will not make room for grief. Churches that are oriented almost entirely toward celebration, victory, breakthrough, praise, and productivity can become suffocating for people who are in seasons of loss, depression, or protracted suffering. The implicit message is clear: Your grief does not belong here. Come back when you have something to celebrate.

The biblical tradition tells a different story. The Psalms are saturated with lament. More than a third of them are expressions of grief, confusion, anger, or abandonment. They were not whispered privately; they were sung communally. The people of God have always brought their suffering into worship, not in spite of their faith but as an expression of it.

A culture of care honors this tradition. It makes room in its worship for the full spectrum of human experience, not only the mountaintops but the valleys too. It allows silence without rushing to fill it. It resists the relentless emphasis on victory and productivity that can make slower seasons of healing feel like spiritual failure.

Healing requires space.

Faith grows where people are allowed to breathe.

A WORD TO THOSE WHO ARE HURTING

If you are longing for a church that feels like what I have described in this chapter, if you can imagine it but have not yet found it, I want to say something directly to you.

Your longing is not naïve. It is not unrealistic. It is not asking for more than the church was designed to offer. The desire to be held in community, to be known without penalty, to bring your whole self into a room and have it received with care, is a deeply biblical desire. It is the desire for the body of Christ to be what its head designed it to be.

You were never meant to carry your pain alone.

You were meant to be held.

Not every church is there yet. The work of becoming a community of genuine care is ongoing, imperfect, and often slow. But it is happening. In the next chapter, we will meet communities that chose to change and see what that change looks like from the inside.

REFLECTION QUESTIONS

1. Think about a time when you felt genuinely safe to be honest in a faith community. What made that safety possible? Who created it, and how?

2. This chapter describes language as forming the emotional climate of a community. What phrases does your church use regularly that might unintentionally minimize pain or police emotion? What could you replace them with?

3. Where does your community currently rely too heavily on a single leader or small group to carry the burden of pastoral care? What would it look like to distribute that responsibility more widely?

4. How does your church currently relate to mental health professionals? Do you have referral relationships, or is professional care treated as separate from the faith community? What first step could you take toward building a bridge?

5. This chapter says lament belongs in worship, not just celebration. Does your community make room for grief? If not, what would it take to create that space?

PART III

FROM
HEALING
TO ACTION

CHAPTER 6

STORIES OF HOPE AND HEALING

Hope begins in the dark, the stubborn hope that if you just show up and try to do the right thing, the dawn will come.

ANNE LAMOTT, *Traveling Mercies*

Hope can feel complicated when you have been disappointed before.

For those who have been hurt in church spaces, stories of change can stir skepticism or grief rather than inspiration. You may have heard promises before—things would be different, the church was learning, you would be safe this time—and been let down. If you find yourself guarded as you read this chapter, that response makes sense. It is not cynicism. It is wisdom earned through experience.

I want to honor that guardedness. What I am going to ask is simpler than setting it aside. Stay with me through these stories. Not because they will resolve every wound or answer every question, but because they are true. These things happened. These communities changed. And if change happened there, it can happen elsewhere.

These stories are not about perfect churches.

They are about brave ones.

They are not stories of instant transformation.

They are stories of slow, relational change, rooted in humility, listening, and courage.

WHEN ONE PERSON IS BELIEVED

I once worked with a longtime ministry leader, a woman who had given decades of her life to the church with extraordinary faithfulness. She had served in almost every capacity imaginable: teaching, leading worship, coordinating care for others, sitting with the grieving. She was the kind of person the church runs on. The kind who shows up early and leaves late and never asks for anything in return.

Quietly, for years, she had been falling apart. She lived with depression, anxiety, and a burnout so deep it had begun to feel like her natural state. She had spent so long believing that service to God meant sacrificing her basic needs (sleep, rest, nourishment, stillness), she no longer recognized what it felt like to be well. Rest, she told me, was a luxury she could not afford.

When she finally found the courage to tell her pastor what she was carrying, she braced herself. She expected disappointment. She expected to be reminded of her responsibilities, offered a Scripture, and sent back to her post. She had seen it happen to others.

Instead, she was met with something she was not prepared for: care. The pastor listened without interrupting. He did not immediately reach for a remedy. He simply stayed present with what she had shared, then told her that her need for rest was not a failure; it was human. He encouraged her to step back from her responsibilities without shame, pointed her toward a therapist, and in the weeks that followed spoke publicly—carefully, without identifying anyone—about the importance of honoring limits.

Slowly, something shifted. Others began to speak up. A worship leader mentioned she was struggling. A small group coordinator quietly acknowledged he had not been okay for a long time. Person by person, a culture that had rewarded endurance over honesty began to change.

It didn't change because of a program, a series, or a strategic initiative.

It changed through permission.

Change often begins exactly there—not in the boardroom or the budget meeting, but in the moment when one person tells the truth and is met with grace instead of correction.

WHEN CHURCHES CHOOSE LISTENING OVER DEFENSIVENESS

There is a particular kind of courage that does not get celebrated enough in church culture. That is, the courage to hear something painful about yourself and not immediately defend against it.

One congregation I know began to notice patterns they could not explain away: burnout among their most committed volunteers, low attendance in leadership meetings, a quiet stream of people leaving without explanation, and disengagement in small groups that had once been vibrant. Rather than attributing these to external factors, leadership chose to ask a hard question: What are we missing?

They created space for honest feedback and committed in advance to listening without defending themselves. What they heard was not comfortable. People did not feel safe bringing their emotional struggles to church, they felt dismissed, they felt hurried toward healing before they were ready, they feared their stories of struggle would be preached from the pulpit, they believed vulnerability carried social risk and expressed that mental health had rarely, if ever, been spoken about from the pulpit with honesty and care.

The leaders sat with that. They did not rush to fix it or explain it away. They acknowledged the harm, expressed genuine remorse, and began the slower work of learning, pursuing training, adjusting how they handled prayer requests, and creating more space for lament alongside celebration.

Trust did not return overnight.

But it did return with time.

And the people who had been quietly slipping away began, cautiously, to come back. Not because everything was perfect, but because they had witnessed something they had not seen before: leadership willing to be wrong, willing to learn, willing to stay in the discomfort long enough to grow through it.

WHEN FAITH AND THERAPY WALK TOGETHER

For a long time, therapy was something people in many churches whispered about, if they mentioned it at all. It carried an unspoken implication: faith had not been sufficient, prayer had run out, and something was broken in a way the church could not address. People who sought therapy often did so quietly, sometimes with shame.

I have watched this narrative change, one conversation at a time.

One of the most profound examples I have witnessed came through a woman who came to me presenting with debilitating and chronic pain. She had been living with it for years. Medications helped manage it but nothing resolved it. As we began to work together, a fuller picture emerged.

She had grown up with a father who was an elder in the church. He was faithfully present in ministry, but faithfully absent at home. He was verbally and physically abusive. He put the church before his family without apology, insisting it was God's design. Her mother, left to raise eight children largely alone, became emotionally exhausted and depressed. When her mother finally found the courage to speak with the pastor about what was happening at home, the response was devastating: the pastor affirmed her husband's position. He told her that her husband's service to God's kingdom was bringing glory to God, and that the family needed to honor that rather than complaining.

My client, the eldest of the eight children, had carried that story in her body for decades. She became angry at God and the church. She left for almost twenty years. And the anger, the grief, the unprocessed trauma of a childhood shaped by religious harm and domestic abuse had nowhere to go. So, it went into her body.

When she started to unpack the trauma in therapy, something remarkable happened. Her chronic pain began to dissipate. She told me that for the first time in her life, she was able to name what she was feeling. She felt safe, in her own body and in the therapeutic environment, to express herself without fear of retaliation, judgment, invalidation, or rejection. The pain, she came to understand, was trauma stuck in her body with nowhere to go. As the trauma found language, as it was witnessed and validated in a safe relationship, the body began to release what it had been holding.

She eventually no longer needed pain medication. She began to attend a local church with a friend, in a community where she felt safe, where she was not required to pretend to be well, and where her full story was welcome. Faith and therapy had walked together toward her healing. Neither alone would have been enough.

A woman I know took a risk during a prayer meeting. She spoke, carefully and with visible hesitation, about how therapy had helped her process childhood trauma she had never felt safe naming in church. She was not sure how it would land. The group leaned in.

Another woman spoke about patterns she had carried since childhood that had shaped her marriage and her sense of worth. A young couple shared the grief of a miscarriage and how a counselor had given them language for what they were experiencing when they had none. A man spoke quietly about his struggle with alcohol abuse, as though he had been waiting years for a room where it would be safe to say it out loud.

One by one, the hidden things came forward. Over time, therapy stopped being something that needed to be whispered about or apologized for. It became part of the ordinary vocabulary of that community. The assumption shifted, slowly but unmistakably, from therapy meaning your faith failed to therapy meaning you are taking your healing seriously.

WHEN LEADERS SPEAK UP

Many pastors are afraid to speak up about their own mental health struggles. They believe that speaking up may lessen their authority, value, or calling. But there is something that happens in a congregation when a leader chooses to be honest about their own struggle. It is difficult to manufacture and impossible to replicate with a sermon series alone.

I know of a pastor of a small congregation, well-loved, deeply committed, who stood at the front of his church one Sunday morning and said something his congregation had never heard from that spot before. He told them he had been living with anxiety for most of his adult life. There were Sunday mornings when he had stood in this same place, preaching about peace, while quietly managing a panic attack. He had finally sought help, and seeking help had not weakened his faith, but had given him more of himself to bring to God and to them.

The room was very still. Then, over the following weeks, something began to happen. A retired schoolteacher told him she had been managing depression for thirty years and had never told anyone at church. A young father admitted he had been struggling since the birth of his second child. This led to the formation of a group where people with lived experience began meeting together. Not as a formal ministry, not with a curriculum, but simply as people who finally felt safe enough to be known.

In another congregation, a leadership team invited a Christian psychologist to speak during a Sunday service on the intersection of faith and mental health. That single sermon led to a three-part series, then a formal partnership with a local counseling center. Today, that church hosts quarterly mental health workshops and includes prayers for emotional healing in every service. People have returned to faith because they finally found healing for the whole person.

None of this began with a strategy. It began with a willingness to speak honestly from the front of the room.

WHEN SURVIVORS SHAPE THE CULTURE

Perhaps the most profound shift I have witnessed is the moment when those who have been most wounded become those who help shape how care is offered.

In one community I know of, several people who had experienced significant trauma, and had, at various points, been harmed by careless church responses to that trauma, were invited into a conversation about how the church could do better. They were not asked to testify about their healing for the sake of an inspiring story. They were asked to teach: To name what had hurt. To describe what safe would have looked like. To help build the language and the practices that might protect others from the same wounds.

The shift in that community, from a culture that managed suffering to one that genuinely accompanied it, was quietly led by the people who had suffered most.

WHAT THESE STORIES SHARE

Looking across these stories, what strikes me is not the programs or the sermons or the strategic decisions. It is the posture. In every case, something changed when a community made a series of quiet, costly choices:

- Humility over image: choosing honesty about failure rather than protecting a reputation

- Listening over explanation: receiving hard things without immediately defending against them

- Presence over performance: staying with people in pain rather than rushing them toward resolution

- Relationship over resolution: trusting that being with someone matters more than fixing them

They stayed when discomfort arose.

They allowed healing to take the time it needed.

And healing came, not as a reward for their effort,

but as the natural consequence of safety finally being offered.

HOPE WITHOUT PRESSURE

If you are still waiting for a church that feels like this, I want to speak to you directly.

You are not wrong to want it. The longing you carry for a community where you are truly known and truly safe is not naïve or unrealistic. It is biblical. It is the longing for the body of Christ to be what Christ designed it to be. That longing is worth honoring. There is hope that you can find your community.

Hope does not require rushing back into spaces that have harmed you.

Hope does not require overriding your instincts to protect yourself.

Hope does not require pretending to believe in change you have not yet seen.

Sometimes hope looks like taking your time.

Sometimes it looks like choosing distance while you heal.

Sometimes it looks like seeking a different community, one where the culture is already closer to what you need.

Sometimes it simply looks like allowing yourself, carefully and without obligation, to believe that change is possible.

That is enough. That is, in fact, a form of faith.

A QUIET INVITATION

These stories are not meant to create expectation or to pressure you toward a particular response. They are meant to create possibility. They remind us that the church is not static, that communities can learn, that leaders can grow, that cultures built on silence and performance can be rebuilt on honesty and care.

You may be the person in your community who is brave enough to tell the truth first. Or you may be the person who is simply trying to survive long enough to find your way to a safer one. Either way, you are not alone in this.

In the next chapter, we will turn toward the practical. We will explore how ordinary believers, without clinical training or formal authority, can become instruments of genuine care for those who are suffering.

REFLECTION QUESTIONS

1. Which story in this chapter resonated most deeply with you (the ministry leader who was finally believed, the church that chose listening over defensiveness, or the prayer group that walked alongside people through professional care)? What did that story open in you?

2. Think of a moment when someone in a faith community chose presence over answers in your own life. What did that mean to you? How did it shape your sense of safety?

3. What is your honest reaction to hope right now? Does it feel accessible, complicated, or out of reach? What has formed that response?

4. This chapter describes change beginning when one person told the truth and was met with grace. Who might that person be in your community? Could it be you?

5. What would you need to consistently see over time to believe that a church culture had genuinely changed? What benchmarks would matter most to you?

CHAPTER 7

EQUIPPING THE SAINTS TO CARE WELL

*The friend who can be silent with us in a moment of
despair or confusion, who can stay with us in an hour
of grief and bereavement, who can tolerate not knowing,
not curing, not healing—that is a friend who cares.*

HENRI J.M. NOUWEN, *The Wounded Healer*

One of the quiet reasons churches avoid conversations about mental health is fear.

Fear of saying the wrong thing.

Fear of not knowing enough.

Fear of making things worse.

I understand that fear. As a psychologist, I have sat with it myself, wondering whether I had the right words; as a minister, wondering whether I was doing more harm than good. The fear of causing harm to someone who is already suffering is not small, and I do not want to minimize it.

But here is what years of walking alongside hurting people has taught me: The fear of imperfect presence is almost never the greatest danger in the room. The greatest danger, almost always, is absence. It is the silence that falls when no one knows what to say and everyone decides that saying nothing is safer. It is the empty chair at the table of someone who needed to be seen and was not.

Harm is far more often caused by dismissal than by imperfect care.

The church does not need everyone to become an expert.

It needs people willing to show up with humility, attentiveness, and love. It needs people willing to stay.

CARE WAS ALWAYS MEANT TO BE COMMUNAL

When we talk about mental health in the church, there is a temptation to place the entire weight of responsibility on pastors and professional counselors. The thinking goes, if the trained people handle it, the rest of us are off the hook.

But Scripture will not allow that division. Paul's image of the church as a body—many parts, each necessary, each responsible for the others—was not a metaphor about organizational efficiency. It was a theology of mutual care. When one part suffers, the whole body responds (1 Corinthians 12:12-27).

Some people are gifted at listening in ways that make others feel genuinely heard.

Some are gifted at noticing or seeing the person who is struggling to hold their smile together.

Some are gifted at practical support, delivering meals, running errands, or simply showing up for others.

Some are gifted at advocacy. They push for language and structures that protect the vulnerable.

Every one of these gifts is essential. Every one is a form of care. And healthy churches recognize that when care is shared across the community, it is both more effective and more sustainable. No single caregiver, however gifted, can carry what a whole body was designed to hold together.

YOU DO NOT NEED A DEGREE TO CARE WELL

I want to say something that I wish someone had said to me earlier in my own journey of trying to care for hurting people: You do not need a clinical degree to show up well for someone who is suffering. You never did. What you need is a willing heart and a few simple understandings about how pain works.

The first is that pain does not always announce itself clearly. The person who is chronically late, perpetually defensive, or quietly pulling away from community may not be difficult. They may be hurting in ways they do not yet have language for. When I learned to ask, "What might be going on beneath this?" rather than "What is wrong with this person?" it changed how I saw almost everyone around me. It will change how you see them too.

The second is that healing cannot be rushed. It belongs to the person doing the healing—on their timeline, not ours. I have watched well-meaning people cause harm simply by moving too fast—by expecting someone to feel better, forgive sooner, or return to fullness on a schedule that felt comfortable to the caregiver. Healing is not a project with a deadline. It is a journey with a companion. Our job is to walk alongside, not to push from behind.

The third is that trust must be earned, not assumed. This is especially true for someone who has been harmed in a church context. Trust is not the starting point, but the destination—arrived at slowly, through consistent and faithful behavior over time. Do not be discouraged if someone holds back. Be faithful and let faithfulness do its quiet work.

And the fourth—the one I come back to again and again in my clinical work and in my own life—is that presence matters more than answers. Most people who are suffering do not primarily need someone to fix them. They need someone to stay. They need to know that what they are carrying will not drive you away. That simple gift, showing up and remaining, is more healing than most of us realize.

When a community begins to hold these things—gently, imperfectly, together—something shifts. Conversations slow down. Responses soften. People stop feeling like problems to be managed and start feeling like human beings to be accompanied. That shift does not require a degree. It requires love.

THE GIFT OF BEING TRULY HEARD

I have been a psychologist for many years, and if there is one thing my training and practice have taught me above everything else, it is this: Most people are not listened to nearly as much as they need to be. Not because those around them do not care, but because real listening is harder than it looks. It requires resisting some of our most deeply ingrained instincts—the instinct to fix, to reframe, to offer the silver lining, to move things along.

Real listening means letting someone finish before you speak. It means sitting with silence when it comes rather than rushing to fill it. It means asking questions that open a door wider rather than questions that nudge someone toward a conclusion you have already reached. It means letting tears fall without immediately reaching for a tissue and a subject change. It means reflecting back what you have heard—"It sounds like you have been carrying this for a very long time"—rather than immediately reinterpreting it through your own framework.

None of this is complicated. But all of it is countercultural in a world, and a church, that tends to reward quick answers and efficient resolutions. Learning to slow down enough to genuinely hear someone is one of the most radical and Christ-like things you can do.

I think of the people who listened to me in my own season of falling apart. They did not say the perfect thing. Some of them said very little at all. But they stayed. They showed up again the next week. They asked how I was and waited for a real answer. They did not look uncomfortable when the answer was hard. That quality of listening—unhurried, unafraid, present—communicated something no words could have: You are not too much for me. I am not going anywhere.

For many who have been dismissed or silenced, especially in church spaces, this quality of listening is not merely comforting, it is reparative. It begins to repair what careless responses broke. It tells the nervous system what the mind has been afraid to believe: It is safe here. You are safe here.

I have watched untrained volunteers in church communities offer this kind of listening and witnessed it change the trajectory of someone's healing. I have also watched trained professionals offer technically correct responses that left people feeling more alone than before. The difference was not expertise. It was genuine care.

KNOWING WHEN TO REFER—AND WHY IT IS THE MOST FAITHFUL THING YOU CAN DO

There is a conversation I have had many times with well-meaning people in ministry. It usually begins with some version of "I don't want to just send them away. I want to help."

I understand that instinct deeply. It comes from love. But I want to gently reframe it. Referring someone to a mental health professional is not sending them away. It is walking them toward help that can reach what you cannot. The most loving, most faithful, most

Christlike response you can sometimes offer is to say, "What you are carrying is real and serious, and I want to make sure you get the kind of support it deserves."

Referral is not failure.

It is stewardship.

It says that I take your wellbeing seriously enough to make sure you receive the best possible care.

Healthy churches normalize referrals to psychologists, therapists, and counselors; to psychiatrists and medical providers; to support groups and crisis resources. They keep lists of trusted professionals and speak about these resources openly, from the pulpit, in small groups, in pastoral conversations, so that seeking professional help feels like a natural and honored part of the community's approach to care.

BOUNDARIES ARE NOT THE ENEMY OF CARE—THEY ARE WHAT SUSTAIN IT

I want to speak honestly about something that does not get discussed enough—the cost of care without limits.

I have watched deeply compassionate people completely burn out because no one ever told them that caring for others required taking care of themselves first. I have watched ministry leaders absorb the pain of their congregations year after year without adequate support and eventually collapse under a weight that was never meant to be carried alone.

Boundaries are not the enemy of care. They are what make care sustainable. Healthy churches teach (explicitly and consistently) that you are allowed to say no, that you cannot carry what was not given to you to carry, that helping does not mean rescuing, and that burnout is not faithfulness. These are not selfish principles. They are protective ones.

You cannot pour from an empty vessel.

And God never asked you to try.

WHEN THE CHURCH DECIDES TO LEARN

One of the most loving things a church can do for its people is decide to learn. Not because learning alone changes everything—it does not. But because it sends an unmistakable message: The people in this room matter enough for us to be equipped to care for them well.

I have seen what happens in a congregation when leaders begin to learn—really learn—about mental health, trauma, and whole-person care. The preaching changes. Not dramatically, but noticeably. The language during prayer times shifts. The way a pastor responds when someone discloses something vulnerable after a Sunday service is different. The culture begins, slowly and almost imperceptibly, to become safer. People feel it before they can name it. And when they finally name it, they say things like, "I don't know what changed, but I feel like I can breathe here now."

That transformation does not require a formal program, though programs can help. It requires leaders who are willing to be students;

who ask questions about mental health rather than assuming they already have the answers; who seek out training in suicide prevention, trauma-informed conversation, and how to refer someone to professional support with grace and without shame; who treat the education of their congregation as an act of pastoral care—because it is.

A WORD TO THOSE WHO FEEL UNQUALIFIED

Before I close this chapter, I want to speak to the person who has been reading and thinking, *This is not for me. I don't know enough. I would probably make things worse.*

I hear you. And I want to say something directly.

You do not need perfect words.

You do not need all the answers.

You do not need to fix anything.

What you need, what the person sitting next to you in pain actually needs from you, is far simpler than expertise. They need to know that you are not afraid of what they are carrying. That you will not disappear when things get hard. That your love for them is not conditional on their recovering on a particular schedule. That you will not leave them to handle their pain alone.

You need willingness.

You need humility.

You need patience.

You need love.

I have seen people with no clinical training whatsoever offer exactly that, and watched it become the beginning of something that could only be called healing for someone who had nearly given up on the possibility of being known.

That is enough to begin. It has always been enough to begin.

A WORD TO THOSE
WHO ARE STILL HURTING

If you are reading this from a place of your own pain, if you are the one who has needed care and found the church ill-equipped to offer it, I want to acknowledge the particular grief of that experience. Being failed by people who were trying to help is its own kind of wound. It does not mean care is impossible. It means the church is still learning.

You are not obligated to be patient with that process.

You are not required to educate anyone.

You are not responsible for fixing what hurt you.

When you do choose to share your story—on your own terms, in your own time, with people you have chosen to trust—I hope you find a room where someone has learned to listen. You deserve nothing less.

In the next chapter, we will move from equipping to action. We will explore what it looks like to translate awareness and care into the daily, embodied practices that actually change a community over time.

REFLECTION QUESTIONS

1. What fear has most held you back from entering into someone else's mental health struggle? Where does that fear come from, and how has it shaped your response?

2. This chapter distinguishes between listening to fix and listening to witness. Think of a recent conversation where someone shared something difficult with you. Which were you doing? What would it have looked like to shift from one to the other?

3. Have you ever referred someone to professional care? If so, what made that feel like love rather than rejection? If not, what made it difficult?

4. This chapter argues that boundaries are what make care sustainable. Where in your own life do you need to establish or honor a boundary to keep giving from a healthy place?

5. What is one concrete, small step you could take this week to be better equipped to care for someone who is struggling?

CHAPTER 8

FROM AWARENESS TO ACTION

Do your little bit of good where you are; it is those little
bits of good put together that overwhelm the world.

ARCHBISHOP DESMOND TUTU

Awareness changes how we see.
Action changes how we live.

I know what it feels like to want to help but not know where to begin. I have stood in that place myself—as a psychologist wondering whether I had the right words, as a minister uncertain whether I was making things better or worse, and as a friend who loved someone deeply but felt completely ill-equipped for what they were carrying. The feeling of wanting to do something but not knowing what to do is not a sign of inadequacy. It is a sign of care. And care—even imperfect, uncertain, halting care—is where this chapter begins.

This chapter is not a call to urgency.

It is a call to faithfulness.

SHOWING UP WITHOUT TAKING OVER

There is a distinction I want to draw carefully, because getting it wrong causes real harm, even when the heart behind it is full of love. It is the difference between being responsible to someone and trying to rescue them.

We are responsible to one another,
but not responsible for one another's healing.

Rescue tries to fix. It carries too much. It eventually collapses.

Responsibility shows up. It stays within its capacity. It points toward greater help when greater help is needed.

I have watched this distinction make all the difference. The people who burned out in ministry were almost always the ones who confused love with rescue—who believed that caring for someone meant carrying everything they carried, that stepping back was a failure of faithfulness, and that asking for help was admitting they were not enough. Love is not the same as rescue. And genuine care—the sustainable kind, the kind that lasts—knows the difference.

PRESENCE AS A PRACTICE

Something I have noticed in communities that do this work well is that care does not begin with a program. It begins in a posture. It begins in how a leader pauses in the hallway when someone seems off. In how a small group creates enough silence that something honest can be said. In how a pastor responds when a phone call comes on a Thursday afternoon from someone who is not okay.

When a community practices presence—genuinely asking how people are and waiting for the real answer, making room for silence, letting stories unfold at their own pace—it creates something that no program alone can manufacture. It creates safety. And safety is the soil in which everything else grows. It says to the person in the room who is holding something heavy, "You do not have to edit your experience to belong here."

SPEAKING UP WHEN IT MATTERS

I want to talk about something that rarely gets named but matters deeply: the quiet courage of speaking up inside a community you love. Not loudly, not confrontationally, but faithfully, in the small moments where something could be different and you are the one who noticed.

Maybe you are sitting in a Sunday service and you hear a phrase from the pulpit that you know would land hard on someone who is struggling. You do not have to stand up. You do not need a platform or a title or permission. You need only the courage to find the pastor afterward and say, gently, "I wonder if there is another way to say that." That is advocacy. That is the kind of quiet faithfulness that changes communities over time.

Maybe it looks like asking your small group leader if there is space for people to share honestly before the prayer requests are collected. Maybe it looks like, suggesting that your church build a referral list of trusted counselors and offering to help. Maybe it looks like sitting with someone who is vulnerable and making sure they are not alone when the community around them does not yet know how to respond well. None of this requires a degree or a title. It requires attentiveness and love—the willingness to notice what others may be missing and the courage to say something, gently and persistently, over time.

CARING FOR YOURSELF IS PART OF THE WORK

I cannot move through this chapter without saying something that is easy to overlook when we are focused on caring for others: the work begins with you. Not in a self-centered sense, but in the most practical, most faithful sense possible.

You cannot offer sustainable care from a depleted self. You cannot model wholeness while privately falling apart. You cannot ask people to honor their limits while quietly violating your own. I have watched this pattern many times in ministry—the person who cared for everyone else until there was nothing left, who mistook exhaustion for devotion and collapse for sacrifice. I have also lived it.

You are not called to ignore your limits.

You are not called to sacrifice your well-being to prove devotion.

You are not called to carry more than is yours to carry.

Caring for your own mental health (seeing a therapist if you need one, setting limits on what you take on, resting when you need to rest, asking for help when you are struggling) is not a detour from the work. It is the work. It is what makes everything else sustainable. And it is one of the most powerful things you can model for a community that is learning to do the same.

PRAYER AS COMPANION, NOT SUBSTITUTE

I want to address something directly because I have seen it cause harm: the use of prayer as a way of bypassing someone's need for professional care.

Prayer is not the problem. Prayer is essential. It is a grounding presence, a source of comfort, a reminder of God's nearness in the darkest places. I pray for the people I serve. I believe in the power and the reality of God's intervention in human suffering. None of that is in question.

What I am naming is something different. It's the moment prayer becomes a way of avoiding the harder, slower, more costly work of genuine care. This happens when someone is in crisis and we pray over them and then consider our responsibility discharged; when a person shares something that clearly requires professional support and we offer a Scripture and a blessing instead of a referral; when prayer becomes a way of closing the conversation rather than accompanying the person through it.

Prayer that takes trauma into account asks before it acts. It does not override someone's "no." It does not demand immediate relief or pressure a particular outcome. It does not replace professional care or serve as a spiritual shortcut around the complexity of human suffering. It walks alongside. It holds space. It stays.

Prayer walks with healing.

It does not rush it.

And it does not do the work that God has given to doctors, therapists, and the slow passage of time.

LETTING THIS BE A LONG OBEDIENCE

Cultural change in the church takes time. More time, usually, than any of us want it to. There will be growth and resistance, progress and missteps, energy and fatigue. There will be meetings where the conversation stalls and moments where someone says something harmful and the room goes quiet and you wonder if anything is actually changing.

It is changing. Slowly, imperfectly, and sometimes invisibly, but it is changing. Every community that has created genuine care did so through the accumulation of exactly these moments: the halting conversations, the mistakes and the apologies that followed, the small shifts in language and practice that nobody celebrated but everyone eventually felt.

Faithfulness looks like continuing gently, even when the work feels slow or unseen. It looks like showing up on Monday after the difficult Sunday. It looks like, trying again after a misstep. It looks like staying, even when staying is hard, because the people in that community are worth staying for.

A WORD TO THE WOUNDED

If you are reading this while still hurting, if you are the person this chapter is ostensibly trying to help and yet you are still waiting for help to arrive, I want to say something carefully and directly:

You are not required to lead this work.

You are not obligated to educate others.

You are not responsible for fixing the church.

Your healing comes first. Participation in the broader work of cultural change is always invitational, never compulsory. You do not owe your story to the movement. You do not need to become a spokesperson for what you have survived. You are allowed to simply receive care, to focus on your own healing, and to let others carry this work for a season while you tend to yourself.

That is not selfishness. That is wisdom. And a church that truly understands what it is doing will not ask more of you than that.

A WORD TO THE CHURCH

This work matters deeply. Not as a ministry initiative or a cultural moment, but because every person sitting in your congregation who is carrying pain in secret is a human being made in the image of God, worthy of the full dignity and care that implies.

The church has always had the capacity for this. Every act of genuine compassion, every moment of honest listening, every referral made with care and without shame, every boundary honored and every burden shared—these are not secular practices borrowed from psychology. They are the church being what it was always designed to be.

When the church becomes emotionally safe, it becomes spiritually credible.

When it honors mental health, it reflects the heart of Christ.

When it stays with people in pain, it becomes a living witness to grace.

In the final chapter, we will look at how this work can be sustained over the long arc of a community's life, so that care does not fade when the initial energy quiets, silence does not return when the momentum stalls, and hope continues to grow even in the slow and ordinary seasons.

REFLECTION QUESTIONS

1. This chapter draws a sharp distinction between rescuing someone and being responsible to them. Where in your own caregiving has the line between those two things blurred? What did that cost you or them?

2. Think about the practice of listening as described in this chapter: asking how people are, allowing honest answers, and letting stories unfold slowly. How does the pace of your church community support or prevent this kind of listening?

3. Have you ever advocated quietly for a change in how your church handles mental health (a word to a leader, a question in a meeting, a suggestion offered carefully)? What happened? If you have not, what has held you back?

4. This chapter says caring for your own mental health is an act of stewardship, not selfishness. How do you currently tend to your own emotional and psychological well-being? What does that need to look like for you to sustain this work?

5. What is one specific action, however small, that you are ready to take in your community as a result of reading this book so far?

CHAPTER 9

SUSTAINING THE WORK WITHOUT LOSING THE SOUL

*A long obedience in the same direction—that is the
name for the kind of spiritual life that endures.*

EUGENE H. PETERSON, *A Long Obedience in the Same Direction*

By the time you reach this chapter, something has already happened.

Whether you came to this book as someone who has suffered in silence, or as a leader trying to understand how to do better, or as someone somewhere in between, you have stayed. You have read words that may have been uncomfortable. You may have recognized yourself in some of the stories of harm. You may have felt the ache of the gap between the church as it sometimes is and the church as it was always meant to be.

That staying matters. It is itself a kind of faithfulness.

But I want to be honest with you about something as we approach the end of this journey together. Beginning this work is easier than sustaining it. The initial momentum of conviction, the clarity that comes after reading something that names what you have always sensed, the energy of a community newly committed to doing better is real, and it is good. But it does not last on its own. Without intention, without humility, without the long patience that genuine cultural change requires, even the most compassionate movements eventually fade, harden, or become what they set out to replace.

This chapter is about the long obedience and what it means to stay aligned with the heart of Christ, not just in the season of fresh commitment, but in the ordinary days that follow: when the energy has quieted, when the work is less visible, and when progress is slow and setbacks are real.

Creating a mentally healthy church is not a moment. It is a way of life.

SUSTAINABILITY BEGINS WITH HUMILITY

The single most important quality that sustains compassionate care over time is not strategy or training or resources, though all of these matter. It is humility.

Humility means remaining teachable long after the initial learning has happened. It means continuing to ask, "What are we missing? Who are we still failing? What do we think we understand that we might actually be getting wrong?" It means resisting the temptation to declare the work finished, the culture transformed, the problem solved. Because in communities of imperfect people caring for other imperfect people, that declaration is never entirely true.

Churches that sustain care for mental health long term share a particular posture: they continue learning, actively invite feedback, admit mistakes without defensiveness, welcome correction from the people they are trying to serve, and resist the cultural pressure to arrive. Humility keeps a community responsive rather than rigid. It allows growth to continue even when discomfort arises.

CARE MUST BE WOVEN INTO EVERYTHING

One of the most common ways mental health initiatives fail in church communities is by remaining separate from the rest of church life: a special program, a designated ministry, or something that happens over here while ordinary church life continues over there. This separation, however well-intentioned, sends an unspoken message: Mental health is a niche concern, relevant to some but not to all.

For care to become a part of culture rather than programming, it must be woven into everything. Into discipleship, where growth is understood to include emotional and psychological wholeness alongside spiritual maturity. Into leadership development, where leaders are trained not only in theology and administration but in self-awareness and the capacity to remain present with suffering. Into pastoral care, preaching and prayer, youth and children's ministry, and the policies and expectations that govern community life. When care is integrated in this way, it stops being something the church does and becomes something the church is.

PROTECTING AGAINST BURNOUT— IN OTHERS AND IN YOURSELF

There is something I need to say frankly because I have watched it happen too many times. Compassionate work done without adequate care for the caregiver eventually becomes harmful. Not immediately and not obviously. It happens gradually. A subtle hardening, a creeping impatience, a growing distance between the care being offered and the genuine warmth that once stimulated it.

This is burnout. And it is not a sign of weakness. It is a sign that a human being has been asked to give more than any human being can sustain without replenishment. Churches committed to long-term care understand this and build protection against it into the structure of their communities. They normalize rest, resist the culture of glorified busyness, offer their leaders sabbaticals as pastoral necessities, and create spaces where those who carry responsibility can set it down for a moment and simply be cared for.

Burnout is not faithfulness.

Sustainability is.

An exhausted caregiver cannot offer safe care. The most faithful thing the church can do for those who are suffering is to ensure that those who serve them are genuinely, sustainably well enough to do so.

CREATING SPACE FOR HONEST FEEDBACK

One of the most important practices for sustaining this work is actively seeking out the stories of people who have been failed by it. Not to dwell in guilt but because the people who have experienced gaps in care carry information that is not available anywhere else. They know where the gaps are because they fell through them. Their experience is not a criticism to be managed. It is data to be honored.

Healthy, sustainable church communities create genuine, ongoing channels for this kind of feedback. This is done through anonymous surveys that make honesty feel safe, listening sessions where leadership commits in advance to receiving without defending, and pastoral relationships where trust has been built slowly enough that honest things can be said. When communities stop listening, they stop growing. And when they stop growing, care eventually calcifies into something that resembles care but no longer genuinely serves.

HONORING HEALING WITHOUT EXPLOITING IT

There is a particular temptation in communities that are doing this work well—one I want to name because it can undermine everything else. It is the temptation to turn people's healing into evidence of the community's success. Someone who was struggling finds genuine care and begins to heal, and is then, subtly or overtly, invited to share their story as a living demonstration of what this church is capable of.

The invitation may be completely sincere. But if the person does not yet have the agency, or the desire to have their healing become a public narrative, the invitation can feel coercive. And it can reopen wounds that were just beginning to close.

Healing is sacred. It belongs entirely to the person who is experiencing it. Sustainable churches allow people to share if and when and how much they choose, without pressure to inspire, educate, or validate the community's efforts.

Not all healing is dramatic.

Much of it is quiet, slow, and deeply holy.

That quiet holiness deserves to be honored on its own terms.

THE WORK THAT NO ONE WILL APPLAUD

I want to close this chapter by honoring something that does not get honored nearly enough. Most of the work that actually changes communities will never be seen.

There will be no applause for the conversation that happened after a Sunday service where a leader took thirty extra minutes to sit with someone who was struggling. There will be no recognition for the referral made quietly and carefully that led to someone finally getting the help they needed. There will be no celebration for the boundary that was held, the harmful phrase that was gently corrected, the meeting where a leader pushed back on an expectation that was burning people out.

There will be no audience for most of the faithfulness this work requires.

Yet, and I believe this with everything in me, God sees it all.

Every conversation that prevented harm.

Every moment of genuine listening that began to rebuild trust.

Every act of referral that honored someone's dignity.

Every silence that made room for grief.

These things are seen. They are counted. They matter in ways that will not always be visible in this life but are real nonetheless. Sustaining this work requires learning to trust that. To find sufficiency in faithfulness itself. Not in outcomes, not in recognition, but in the steady, patient, daily choice to show up for people in pain and to do so with as much care and humility as you can bring.

That is the long obedience. That is what love looks like in a compassionate church when it stops being a feeling and becomes a practice.

A WORD TO LEADERS

You do not have to carry this alone.

I know the weight of leadership in this space. The feeling that the health of everyone else depends on you staying strong, staying available, staying well even when you are not. But I want to say this as directly and as tenderly as I can: The most important thing you can model for your community is not strength. It is honesty. Not the performance of having it together, but the genuine, human, sometimes uncomfortable truth of what it actually costs to do this work, and the courage to seek the care you need to keep doing it well.

Invite support, not as a sign of weakness but as an act of wisdom.

Share leadership, not because you cannot handle it but because you were never meant to carry it alone.

Know your limits, not as a failure of calling but as evidence of humanity.

Model the wholeness you are inviting others into.

The church does not need flawless leaders.

It needs honest ones.

It always has.

A WORD TO THE WOUNDED

If you are still healing, if you are still searching for a community where it is genuinely safe to tell the truth about what you are carrying, I want to leave you with this:

You are not behind.

You are not failing.

You are not forgotten.

The pace of your healing belongs to you. The timing of your trust belongs to you. The choice of when and whether and how much to share belongs entirely to you. Your story is not over. Your belonging has not been revoked. And the God who has been present in every page of this book is present still—not at a distance, not in theory, but right here, in whatever it is you are carrying today.

STAYING THE COURSE

This book does not offer a finish line. It offers a way forward.

Not a way that is easy or fast or free of setbacks, but a way that is faithful. The kind of faithfulness that keeps showing up, keeps learning, keeps choosing presence over performance and love over efficiency.

May the church continue to become a place where:

- Suffering is met with compassion rather than correction.

- Mental health is spoken of with honesty rather than with shame.

- Healing is supported at whatever pace it needs to take.

- Faith is gentle with the struggling rather than demanding of the strong.

- Silence is broken, one honest conversation at a time.

- No one is ever asked to walk alone again.

Let us not grow weary in doing good. Because love practiced faithfully, offered gently, and sustained over the long arc of a life and a community, changes everything (1 Corinthians 13:7).

It always has. It always will.

REFLECTION QUESTIONS

1. This chapter speaks of a gap between the church's initial energy for change and the long, ordinary work of sustaining it. Where have you seen that gap in your own community or ministry? What caused the momentum to fade?

2. What personal practices (spiritual, relational, physical) currently sustain you in this kind of work? What is missing, and what would it take to add it?

3. This chapter addresses the invisible labor of those who care without recognition. Who in your community does that work unseen? How could you honor and support them this week?

4. What does "faithfulness" look like for you specifically as you close this book? Not as a general ideal, but as a concrete next step in your particular context?

5. If you could make one thing different in your church, your family, or your own heart as a result of everything in this book, what would it be? What is one step you can take toward that goal today?

A CHURCH WHERE HEALING CAN BREATHE

If you are closing this book feeling reflective or quietly emotional, that is not accidental.

This work touches places that have been guarded for a long time—places shaped by silence, misunderstanding, longing, and hope. Trauma-informed healing does not rush those places. It honors them.

This book was never meant to offer quick answers or perfect solutions. It was written to tell the truth with care—about mental health, about faith, and about what it means to belong to one another in the presence of pain.

TO THOSE WHO ARE SUFFERING

If you live with anxiety, depression, trauma, grief, or emotional exhaustion—and have felt unseen or unsafe in church spaces—please hear this clearly:

You are not weak.

You are not broken.

You are not failing God.

Your pain is not a spiritual deficiency.

It is a human experience deserving of care, dignity, and compassion.

You do not owe your story to anyone.

You do not need to rush your healing.

You do not have to remain in unsafe spaces to prove your faith.

God is not waiting for you to become stronger.

God is already near.

> *"The righteous person may have many troubles,*
> *but the Lord delivers him from them all."*
>
> **PSALM 34:19**

Scripture does not deny hardship; it normalizes it. Yet it also promises that God's presence does not abandon the afflicted. Deliverance is not always immediate, and healing is not always linear, but the Lord remains near. Honest faith is not fragile faith. It is faith without shame.

TO THE CHURCH

The church was never meant to be a place of performance or perfection. It was meant to be a place of presence.

A place where people are allowed to be human.

A place where grief is honored rather than rushed.

A place where faith makes room for fragility.

Becoming a compassionate church does not mean abandoning Scripture or conviction. It means embodying the compassion of Christ more fully, especially toward those who have carried invisible wounds for far too long.

Healing begins when the church listens.

When it slows down.

When it chooses relationships over answers.

When it stays.

HOPE WITHOUT PRESSURE

Hope does not require denial.

It does not demand resolution.

It does not insist that everything be okay.

Hope can be quiet.

Hope can be slow.

Hope can look like choosing safety.

Hope can look like rest.

Sometimes hope is simply knowing that you are not alone anymore.

A WAY FORWARD

This book is not an ending.

It is an invitation.

An invitation to

- speak with greater care;
- listen with deeper humility;
- lead with wisdom rather than certainty; and
- love with gentleness rather than urgency.

Healing without shame is not about erasing pain. It is about removing the burden of hiding it. It is about creating communities where honesty is not punished, where weakness is not spiritualized, and where grace is not rationed.

It is an invitation for the church to become a place where healing can happen, not because pain disappears, but because people are no longer asked to carry it alone.

A FINAL BLESSING

May we become communities that make room.

May we become churches that stay.

May we become people who understand that healing requires time, safety, and love.

And may grace meet us, body, soul, and spirit, exactly where we are.

REFERENCES

The following works informed the research, theology, and clinical frameworks explored in this book. Readers are encouraged to engage these sources directly for deeper study.

SCRIPTURE

All Scripture quotations are taken from The Holy Bible, New International Version®, NIV®. Copyright © 1973, 1978, 1984, 2011 by Biblica, Inc. Used with permission of Zondervan. All rights reserved worldwide. www.zondervan.com.

MENTAL HEALTH AND TRAUMA

American Psychiatric Association. *Diagnostic and Statistical Manual of Mental Disorders, Fifth Edition, Text Revision.* American Psychiatric Publishing, 2022.

Herman, Judith L. *Trauma and Recovery: The Aftermath of Violence— From Domestic Abuse to Political Terror.* Basic Books, 2022.

Levine, Peter A. *In An Unspoken Voice: How the Body Releases Trauma and Restores Goodness.* North Atlantic Books, 2010.

Maté, Gabor. *When the Body Says No: Exploring the Stress-Disease Connection.* Wiley, 2019.

Porges, Stephen W. *The Polyvagal Theory: Neurophysiological Foundations of Emotions, Attachment, Communication, and Self-regulation.* Norton Series on Interpersonal Neurobiology. W. W. Norton & Company, 2011.

Van der Kolk, Bessel. *The Body Keeps the Score: Brain, Mind, and Body in the Healing of Trauma.* Viking, 2014.

FAITH, THEOLOGY, AND MENTAL HEALTH

Allender, Dan B. *The Wounded Heart: Hope for Adult Victims of Childhood Sexual Abuse.* NavPress, 2008.

Clinton, Tim, and Ron Hawkins. *The Quick-Reference Guide to Biblical Counseling.* Baker Books, 2011.

Langberg, Diane. *Suffering and the Heart of God: How Trauma Destroys and Christ Restores.* New Growth Press, 2015

Langberg, Diane. *Redeeming Power: Understanding Authority and Abuse in the Church.* Brazos Press, 2020.

Scazzero, Peter. *Emotionally Healthy Spirituality: It's Impossible to Be Spiritually Mature While Remaining Emotionally Immature.* Zondervan, 2017.

Smedes, Lewis B. Shame and Grace: Healing the Shame We Don't Deserve. HarperOne, 1996.

Tan, Siang-Yang. *Counseling and Psychotherapy: A Christian Perspective*. Baker Academic, 2011.

TRAUMA-INFORMED CARE AND COMMUNITY

Harris, Maxine, & Roger D. Fallot, R., eds. "Using Trauma Theory to Design Service Systems," *New Directions for Mental Health Services*, no. 3 (April 2001).

Substance Abuse and Mental Health Services Administration (SAMHSA). "SAMHSA's Concept of Trauma and Guidance for a Trauma-Informed Approach," *HHS Publication*, no. SMA 14-4884 (2014). https://www.health.ny.gov/health_care/medicaid/program/medicaid_health_homes/docs/samhsa_trauma_concept_paper.pdf.

Sweeney, Angela, Beth Filson, Angela Kennedy, Lucie Collinson, and Steve Gillard. "A Paradigm Shift: Relationships in Trauma-Informed Mental Health Services." *BJPsych Advances,* 24, no. 5, 319–333. https://doi.org/10.1192/bja.2018.29.

RESOURCES

If you or someone you love is struggling with mental health challenges, please know that help is available. You do not have to navigate this alone. The following organizations offer support, information, and connection to care.

CRISIS SUPPORT

988 Suicide and Crisis Lifeline
Call or text 988 (United States)
www.988lifeline.org.
Available 24 hours a day, 7 days a week. Free and confidential support for people in distress.

Crisis Text Line
Text HOME to 741741 (United States) www.crisistextline.org.
Free, 24/7 crisis counseling via text message.

International Association for Suicide Prevention
www.iasp.info/resources/Crisis_Centres
Directory of crisis centers worldwide.

MENTAL HEALTH SUPPORT

NATIONAL ALLIANCE ON MENTAL ILLNESS (NAMI) HELPLINE

1-800-950-NAMI (6264)

www.nami.org.

Education, advocacy, and support for individuals and families affected by mental illness.

MENTAL HEALTH AMERICA

www.mhanational.org.

Screening tools, resources, and connection to local mental health services.

PSYCHOLOGY TODAY THERAPIST FINDER

www.psychologytoday.com/us/therapists

Searchable directory of licensed therapists, including filters for faith-based care and specialties.

OPEN PATH COLLECTIVE

www.openpathcollective.org

Affordable therapy for individuals, couples, and families ($30–$80 per session).

SUBSTANCE ABUSE AND MENTAL HEALTH SERVICES ADMINISTRATION (SAMHSA)

www.samhsa.gov

Evidence-based resources and trauma-informed care frameworks for organizations and communities.

Suicide Prevention Alliance

www.suicidepreventionalliance.org

A non-profit organization solely dedicated to preventing suicide across the country.

Therapist Aid

www.therapistaid.com

Free worksheets, guides, and psychoeducation materials for individuals and ministry leaders.

FAITH-BASED MENTAL HEALTH RESOURCES

American Association of Christian Counselors (AACC)

www.aacc.net

Directory of Christian counselors and mental health resources for individuals and churches.

Focus on the Family Counseling

1-855-771-HELP (4357).

www.focusonthefamily.com/get-help

Free consultation and referral to Christian counselors.

The Allender Center

www.theallendercenter.org

Resources and training for trauma-informed, faith-integrated care.

FOR CHURCHES
AND MINISTRY LEADERS

MENTAL HEALTH GRACE ALLIANCE.

www.mentalhealthgracealliance.org

Church-based mental health programs, leader training, and congregational support resources.

FRESH HOPE FOR MENTAL HEALTH

www.freshhope.us

Peer-to-peer support groups for people living with mental health challenges, designed for church communities.

SAFE CHURCH TRAINING (various denominations)

Many denominations offer trauma-informed pastoral care training. Contact your denominational headquarters or visit their website for available resources.

If you are in immediate danger, please call
emergency services (911 in the United States)
or go to your nearest emergency room.

ABOUT THE AUTHOR

Dr. Williametta Simmons is a psychologist, entrepreneur, and humanitarian committed to wise, compassionate care, faith-based healing, and community wellness.

She holds a Doctorate in Psychology and an MBA and is the founder of Integrative Psychological & Consulting Services, LLC.

Born in Liberia and raised in the United States, her work bridges clinical excellence, cultural humility, and spiritual compassion. She is a dedicated member of the Liberia Medical Mission team, bringing mental health resources and humanitarian care to West Africa.

Dr. Simmons is a sought-after speaker, ministry leader, and advocate for the integration of faith and mental health. She writes and speaks with the authority of both professional training and lived experience, offering hope to those who have suffered in silence and equipping faith communities to become places of genuine healing.

WWW.HEALINGWITHOUTSHAME.COM

www.ingramcontent.com/pod-product-compliance
Lightning Source LLC
Chambersburg PA
CBHW031142130726

47988CB00006B/2484